# PHYSIOLOGY OF AGING
## A SYNOPSIS

# PHYSIOLOGY OF AGING
## A SYNOPSIS

**RICHARD A. KENNEY, Ph.D.**

*Professor and Chairman*
*Department of Physiology*
*George Washington University*
*School of Medicine and Health Sciences*
*Washington, D.C.*

YEAR BOOK MEDICAL PUBLISHERS, INC.
CHICAGO • LONDON

**Library of Congress Cataloging in Publication Data**

Kenney, Richard A.
    Physiology of aging.

    Includes bibliographies and index.
    1. Aging. 2. Age factors in diseases. I. Title.
[DNLM: 1. Aging. WT 104 K36p]
QP86.K46        612'.67        82-4731
ISBN 0-8151-5016-4                AACR2

*This book is dedicated to my wife, BETTE,
for every possible reason.*

# Contents

Preface . . . . . . . . . . . . . . . . . . . xi


PART I  GENERAL ASPECTS OF AGING . . . . . . .  1

1 / Introduction—Aging in man . . . . . . . . . .  3
    The Aging Population . . . . . . . . . . . . .  3
    Human Life Span . . . . . . . . . . . . . .  4
    Life Span Potential . . . . . . . . . . . . .  5
    Man as a Special Case of Aging . . . . . . . .  7
    The Study of Aging in Man . . . . . . . . . .  8

2 / The Aging Process . . . . . . . . . . . . . .  11
    Aging as the Impairment of Homeostasis . . . . . .  11
    Aging as an Immune Phenomenon . . . . . . . .  12
    Cellular Aspects of Aging . . . . . . . . . .  14
    The Study of Cellular Aging . . . . . . . . . .  15
    Theories of Aging . . . . . . . . . . . . .  17
    Free Radicals and Aging . . . . . . . . . . .  19

3 / Aging Changes in Body Conformation and
Composition . . . . . . . . . . . . . . . . .  21
    Body Conformation . . . . . . . . . . . . .  21
    Body Composition . . . . . . . . . . . . . .  22


PART II  AGING OF TISSUES AND ORGAN SYSTEMS . .  29

4 / Blood, Supporting Tissues, Muscle, Skin,
and Teeth . . . . . . . . . . . . . . . . . .  31
    Blood . . . . . . . . . . . . . . . . . .  31
    Supporting Tissues . . . . . . . . . . . . .  32
    Muscle . . . . . . . . . . . . . . . . . .  36

Skin and Appendages . . . . . . . . . . . 37
Teeth and Oral Structures . . . . . . . . . . 38

**5 / The Respiratory System, the Cardiovascular System, and Physical Activity in Aging** . . . . . . . . . . **42**
Respiratory System . . . . . . . . . . . 42
Cardiovascular System . . . . . . . . . . 48
Physical Activity in Aging . . . . . . . . . 52

**6 / The Kidney and the Alimentary Tract** . . . . . . **56**
Kidney . . . . . . . . . . . . . . . 56
Alimentary Tract . . . . . . . . . . . . 60

**7 / The Nervous System** . . . . . . . . . . . . **65**
Anatomical Aging of the Brain . . . . . . . . 65
Cellular Changes . . . . . . . . . . . . 65
Cerebral Blood Flow . . . . . . . . . . . 68
Neurotransmitters . . . . . . . . . . . . 68
Aging of Reflexes . . . . . . . . . . . . 70
Reaction Time . . . . . . . . . . . . . 71
Aging of the Senses . . . . . . . . . . . 71
Vestibular Function . . . . . . . . . . . 76
Balance and Posture . . . . . . . . . . . 77
Gait . . . . . . . . . . . . . . . . 77
Tremor . . . . . . . . . . . . . . . 77

**8 / The Endocrine System and the Reproductive System** . **80**
The Endocrine System . . . . . . . . . . . 80
The Reproductive System . . . . . . . . . . 84

**9 / Aging of Regulatory Mechanisms** . . . . . . . . **90**
Autonomic Nervous System . . . . . . . . . 90
Aging Changes in Homeostatic Regulation . . . . . 91
Aging of Homeostatic Mechanisms . . . . . . . 91

**PART III   OTHER CONSEQUENCES OF AGING** . . . . **99**

**10 / Aging Changes in Higher Functions** . . . . . . . **101**
The Aging EEG . . . . . . . . . . . . . 101
Averaged Evoked Potentials (AEP) . . . . . . . 102

Sleep . . . . . . . . . . . . . . . 103
Dreaming . . . . . . . . . . . . . 105
Memory and Learning . . . . . . . . . . 105

**11 / Nutrition, Drugs, and Biologic Age** . . . . . . . . **109**
Nutrition in Aging . . . . . . . . . . . . 109
Drugs and the Aged . . . . . . . . . . . 112
Biologic Age . . . . . . . . . . . . . . 115

**Index** . . . . . . . . . . . . . . . . . . **119**

# Preface

THIS BOOK presumes its readers are already familiar with normal physiology, the focus of most "core" courses in the subject. It offers a concise description of the functional changes that occur as a part of the normal course of aging, and distinguishes these normal changes from specific pathologic processes that occur with increasing frequency as an individual ages.

With an increasing percentage of the population reaching old age, the health care practitioner must be able to recognize the changing parameters of health in the old and avoid the mistaken interpretation of these changes as disease. Some of the changes that occur are major and obvious; others are more subtle; and some can be slowed in their occurrence by an appropriate lifestyle.

Slowing those changes is both realistic and worthwhile, for the clock of biologic aging is not synchronized with the passage of years. It is the geriatrician's role to slow that clock relative to chronological time. To date, medicine has made enormous strides in adding years to life; the challenge for the future will be to add life to those years. Meeting that challenge requires an understanding of the special features of healthy function in this growing segment of society. The text that follows endeavors to stimulate that understanding.

In order to be concise I have been dogmatic, and only occasionally are statements supported by citation of the experimental evidence. Where specific data have been used in the construction of an illustration, appropriate reference is made. A list of suggested readings follows each chapter.

## Acknowledgments

It is a pleasure to acknowledge the contribution made by so many to the development of this small book. Drs. L. Thompson Bowles and Robert G. Brown ignited my interest in the topic of aging; my colleagues let me use them as sounding boards for my ideas; the medical students and students in the Gerontology Program inspired the effort to write a text.

My unreserved thanks are due to Selma Klein, who by her skilled and patient secretarial work made the preparation of the manuscript a pleasure, and to the editorial staff of Year Book Medical Publishers for their advice and encouragement throughout.

RICHARD A. KENNEY

# PART I

# GENERAL ASPECTS OF AGING

# 1 / Introduction—Aging in Man

AGING is an integral part of the process of growth and development that is terminated by death. Animals in the wild seldom have the opportunity to show the changes of senility; loss of muscle power, diminution of visual acuity, and other deterioration make the aging beast relatively easy prey. The protection of society and the support afforded by technology, however, enable man to survive, and we are moving at an accelerating pace toward an older society.

## The Aging Population

There are 25 million persons in the United States aged 65 or older. In this century, the number of people in this age group has increased eightfold. In 1900, persons aged 65 and over constituted 4% of the population, whereas today the figure is 11%. By the year 2000, it is estimated that one of every eight members of the population will be older than 65. In 1900, approximately one fourth of those who lived to be age 65 reached age 75; in the year 2000, this fraction will approach one half.

The sex ratio in the older population has also changed in a striking way. In 1900, there were 102 older men for every 100 older women; today, there are nearly 150 older women for every 100 older men. In the over-75 age group, the ratio is 180 women for every 100 men.

The increased numbers of older persons in our society result from three factors: (1) high birth rates in the early years of this century, (2) large numbers of immigrants entering the society in the years before World War I and between the world wars, and (3) an increase in life expectancy.

---

The demographic data cited are taken from publications of the White House Conference on Aging.

## Human Life Span

The life expectancy of young people is increasing at a much faster rate than that of older persons. In 1900, only 39% of those born could be expected to reach age 65; today, the figure is nearly 75%. On the other hand, a third of those who reached age 65 in 1900 could expect to live to be 80; today, that fraction has risen to only one half. A comparison of the survivorship curves for 1900 and 1980 reveals major changes (Fig 1–1). The substantial decrease in the percent surviving in the early and middle years has largely disappeared. However, the extreme right end of the curve has remained essentially fixed. In other words, the trend is not toward a population with an increasing number of centenarians but rather toward increasing numbers of people surviving the young adult and middle years to approach more nearly their full potential life span. Viewed in the longer term, this effect is striking. At the start of the Christian era, the average age at death was probably around 30 years; at the start of this century, it was 50 years; today it is nearly 75 and yet those who survive the longest live no longer today than they did 2,000 years ago. (The book of Joshua in the Bible states, "Moses was a hundred and twenty when he died: his eye was not dim nor his natural force abated.")

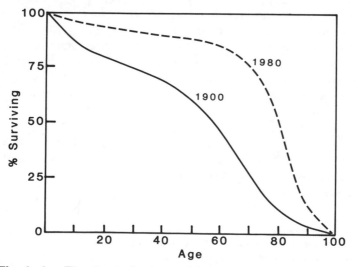

**Fig. 1–1.**—The change in shape of the survivorship curve from 1900 to 1980.

## Life Span Potential

The survivorship curves suggest that the maximum achievable life span is a characteristic of the species and reflects a characteristic rate of aging. Cutler (1976) has studied the issue of maximal life span potential from an evolutionary point of view and has concluded that the rate of aging has remained essentially unchanged for the past 100,000 years. The study of hominid evolution suggests that over the course of 3 million years the potential life span has doubled. During this time the rate of increase at first accelerated, but 100,000 years ago the increase stopped and the potential life span became fixed. Brain size increased over a similar time course, and this has led to the notion that the brain plays some central role in the aging process.

It may be appropriate to specify in broad terms the different varieties of death that terminate the process of aging.

1. Trauma and accidents are the major causes of death in young adulthood. The rate of this premature loss is determined largely by the extent to which society will accept regulation to diminish the risks occasioned by, for example, high-speed vehicles, dangerous occupations, or life-shortening habits such as substance abuse or smoking.

2. Another cause is disease processes that have overwhelmed the defense or repair systems of the body. The past 100 years have seen a striking reduction in the number of deaths of this kind, as understanding of the basis of disease has developed and prevention and therapy have been instituted. It is probably not overly optimistic, therefore, to regard such deaths as "premature." Many diseases that led to death in the neonatal period have been conquered. Now the majority of deaths from disease occur in the elderly, in whom diminished functions can tolerate less accumulation of pathology than in the young. Some disease processes occur almost exclusively in the old, and this linkage of specific pathology and old age justifies the use of the term "pathogeric" to describe such processes. Nonetheless, deaths from pathogeric causes can properly be included in the category of preventable and, therefore, premature death.

3. If there were no deaths from trauma and disease were totally eliminated, man would still die as a consequence of a reduced

ability to maintain an equitable internal environment in the face of external environmental stresses. This decreased ability to maintain homeostasis as one ages is universal. Since it involves no specific pathology, it can be called a "eugeric" change (leading to eugeric death). Paton (1954), in a delightful description of an individual in whom all the regulatory functions provided by the autonomic nervous system were blocked by the drug hexamethonium, speculated that death would ultimately come from increasing entropy of the unregulated system. Eugeric death and entropy death have much in common. It might be assumed that the rates of failure of homeostatic competence would show a normal distribution, since many components of the regulatory complexes exhibit a linear decrease in function with age. On this basis, one might draw an ideal survivorship curve with a value of about 85 as the mean age at death for those surviving accidental death (Fig 1–2). The concepts of "aging, natural death, and the compression of morbidity" have been reviewed by Fries (1980), who points out the implications of this changing pattern of survivorship for society, for research on aging, and for the practice of medicine.

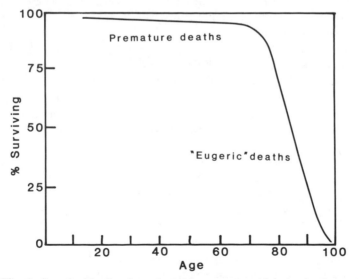

Fig. 1–2.—An idealized survivorship curve in which randomly occurring death by accident is the only cause of premature death and deaths from old age are normally distributed about a mean age of 85.

There have been reports of special groups of individuals who are exceptionally long-lived. Claims of ages of 150 to 160 have been made for groups in Ecuador and in Georgian Russia, but there are major doubts about the authenticity of these claims (Mazess and Forman, 1979). Recently a technique of protein-dating has been developed that will be useful to test such claims of longevity. It is based on the fact that amino acids once laid down in protein undergo a progressive racemization with time. While most proteins are dynamic throughout life with a recycling of the amino acids, a few proteins, once laid down, do not undergo recycling. Tooth protein and the protein of the lens of the eye are two examples. By estimating the degree of racemization of the amino acids in teeth that have to be extracted or in a lens removed because of a cataract, scientists may resolve the controversies presently surrounding the claims of great age.

The division of a population into "young," "adult," "middle-aged," and "old" is frequently based on personal stereotypes and is highly colored by one's own position on the scale. The World Health Organization has developed a classification in which the "elderly" are those aged 60 to 75, the "old" aged 76 to 90, and the "very old" over age 90. This classification, however, has a limited value in describing the physiology of the process of aging, since biologic aging is a plastic process. Many changes that are regarded as eugeric in the sense that they appear universal in populations can be prevented or retarded in particular individuals by the adoption of appropriate life-styles. To cite one example, the decreased ability to use oxygen in old age can be kept to a minimum with a regimen of regular exercise. The range of abilities to use oxygen may be far greater among individual members of an age group than among groups of individuals separated in age by 20 to 30 years.

## Man as a Special Case of Aging

In the vertebrate animals, a number of factors show some correlation with life span. There is an inverse correlation between life span and rate of metabolism, there is a direct correlation with the length of the growth period, and there is some direct correlation with body weight. On these bases, especially the latter, man appears to be an exception; his life span is longer than would be predicted. If brain weight is considered, however, the correlation improves and man is no longer an exception. Conceivably, a large brain may make for an extended life span either by providing for a more effective, intelligent interaction with the environment or by providing more precise homeostatic control. However, there is no evidence that homeostatic control is any less precise in the chimpanzee than in man, and their life spans differ by a factor of two. Furthermore, the relatively strong correlation ($r = 0.80$) between life span and brain weight is not unique; the adrenal gland weight exhibits the same relationship.

Man is also an exception to the general rule in that his life span extends well beyond the reproductive period. This is not particularly advantageous from the viewpoint of evolutionary efficiency, since it results in an increased drain on society's resources without a matching increase in the opportunity for species adaptation by genetic combination. Because a large brain does not make man more homeostatically efficient, its advantage must relate to the external rather than to the internal environment. The ability to accumulate information and communicate it within the species, which is provided by a large brain, justifies the long postreproductive life but does not explain how longevity is achieved. Although the result of aging is loss of the ability to withstand stress, the fundamental processes must be examined at levels below that of the whole organism—at the level of organs or specific tissues or at the cellular and molecular level.

## The Study of Aging in Man

The two basic approaches to the study of human aging are the *cross-sectional study* and the *longitudinal study*. In the former, a population with a broad span of ages (perhaps birth to 90 years) is "sectioned" into narrow age-defined subsets and measurements are made in an identical fashion in each group. In the longitudinal study, a population is identified at an early age and measurements are made on the group at specific time intervals so that the process of aging can be examined in a dynamic fashion.

The cross-sectional study, although less time-consuming, is subject to a number of errors. Among these are the so-called secular changes—changes that occur in the population as a whole over time. An example is stature. For a variety of reasons, some genetic and some environmental, the 20-year-old in 1980 is taller than was the 20-year-old in 1910. If there were no loss of stature with age, a cross-sectional study would lead to the erroneous conclusion that as individuals age, their body height decreases (Fig 1–3). Another problem arises from *differential survivorship,* by which only individuals who show (or lack) a particular characteristic survive to contribute to the observations in older age groups. To continue the example of stature, it is possible that tall, lean individuals tend to live longer than the short and obese; if true, this would bias the outcome of the study.

The longitudinal study avoids the grossest of these errors, but it is difficult to apply to man since the time required by the study is also the life span of the observer. Furthermore, it calls for a very stable (and dedicated) population. A compromise between the cross-sectional and the longitudinal studies is the so-called semi-longitudinal approach, in which groups that overlap in age composition are studied for a limited number of years.

A study of human aging has other inherent problems. First, one must use informed volunteer subjects, and the nature of the invi-

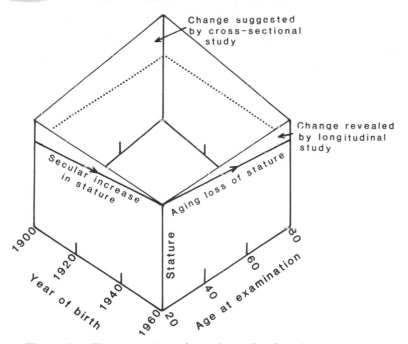

**Fig. 1–3.**—The interaction of secular and aging changes as examined by cross-sectional and longitudinal studies.

tation may result in the recruitment of a group that is not representative of the whole, perhaps by being especially attractive to the health-conscious individual or to the hypochondriac. Second, ethical limitations on human experimentation constrain the studies that can be undertaken. Third, secular or individual differences in life-style, diet, smoking, and other habits can confound studies that extend over a significant time. For these reasons, much of the information on the dynamic aspects of aging is necessarily derived from short-lived species.

## SUGGESTED READING

Comfort A.: Aging: The Biology of Senescence. New York, Elsevier North-Holland, Inc., 1978.

Cutler R.G.: Evolution of longevity in primates. J. Hum. Evol. 5:169–202, 1976.

Economas A.C.: Brain-life span conjecture: A re-evaluation of the evidence. Gerontology 26:82–89, 1980.

Fries J.F.: Aging, natural death and the compression of morbidity. N. Engl. J. Med. 303:130–135, 1980.

Kent S.: The evolution of longevity. Geriatrics 35(1):98–104, 1980.

Mazess R.B., Forman S.H.: Longevity and age exaggeration in Vilcabomba, Ecuador. J. Gerontol. 34:94–98, 1979.

Paton W.D.M.: Transmission and block in autonomic ganglia. Pharmacol. Rev. 6:66, 1954.

# 2 / The Aging Process

AGING may be defined as the sum of all the changes that occur in man with the passage of time and lead to functional impairment and death. An alternative definition might be a decreasing ability to survive stress. Such a definition directs attention to the defense systems of the body—on the one hand, the finely regulated mechanisms that control the internal environment to produce homeostasis and, on the other, the defense mechanisms of the immune system.

## Aging as the Impairment of Homeostasis

Stress may be regarded as any factor or process that tends to shift the internal environment away from its normal equilibrium. In reaction to stress, the body calls into operation a whole array of regulatory processes that have the common objective of restoring equilibrium. The basic components of such systems are devices for the acquisition of information; systems of communication, in our case nerves or humoral, blood-borne information; regulatory centers where comparisons can be made between the current status of a particular variable and the desired target value of that variable; and finally an effector system by which the necessary correction can be made. These elements form a closed loop that engineers would term a "feedback" system. Since the result of the operation is to reduce the amount of deviation of the variable from its target value it is referred to as negative feedback.

The effectiveness of a homeostatic mechanism is judged by how accurately and how completely it can correct a perturbation caused by stress. It is typical for these corrections to occur more slowly in the older person than in the young. For example, following the administration of a test dose, the blood glucose level remains elevated for a longer time in an older person. The heart rate, which is elevated in response to physical activity, returns only slowly to the resting level. The older individual is also less able to adapt to continued stress than the young person. This is seen in acclimatization to high temperatures or to high altitudes, where the disadvantage of age is considerable. In general, regulation or adaptation is impaired in the effector part of the control loop, although in some situations (such as thermoregulation), fault also lies in the precision of the central system. The end point of homeostatic impairment is an internal environment that is incompatible with life.

## Aging as an Immune Phenomenon

The immune system, which is distributed throughout the body and interacts with all other systems, provides another aspect of defense of the internal environment. The immune system ages, and as it does so, immunologic efficiency decreases. As a consequence, there is an increasing incidence of infections, autoimmune diseases, and cancer. In addition, more subtle immune reactions may occur in a widespread fashion throughout the tissues, producing damage to blood vessels and parenchyma, which is expressed in a general impairment of function.

With increasing age, lymphoid tissue is lost from the thymus, spleen, lymph nodes, and bone marrow. In fact, the involution of the thymus gland, which begins in childhood, was noted by Galen as the earliest sign of aging. The loss of lymphoid tissue together with decreased vigor of the remaining stem cells reduces the cellular traffic of the immune system. Present evidence suggests that the major change in the system is in the T-cells, which require thymic activity for their production from pre-T-cells. This may involve the terminal differentiation of the T-cells, thus leading to an imbalance between effector and suppressor functions. Changes in the B-cells, which are responsible for the humoral immune response, are smaller and generally secondary to changes in the T-cell population. Tests of T-cell function using hypersensitivity to antigens to which individuals have previously been sensitized have given equivocal results. However, the decline in function is more apparent in a test of delayed skin reaction to novel antigens or to challenge with tumor cells.

A number of immunologic models of aging have been proposed. One of these, put forward by Walford (1974), is the chronic graft versus host reaction, which resembles the aging process in that both show depletion of lymphoid tissue, thymic involution, renal atrophy, autoantibodies, and widespread deposition of amyloid material, which consists in large part of the light chains of immunoglobulin. A second model of aging is the thymectomized animal, which shows accelerated aging and a shortened life span. The thymus is clearly central to all the changes in the aging immune system. Burnet (1970) has described the thymus as the body's "aging clock." Although the lymphoid tissue of the gland atrophies, the endocrine cells of the medulla remain and the hormone(s) thymosin can be detected in the blood of even old individuals. There is a profound decline in the circulating levels beginning at about puberty and continuing to age 50. Thereafter, the rate of decline slows considerably.

There is interaction between the hypothalamo-pituitary axis and the immune system. Growth hormone and insulin act on T-cell function; thyroxine and the sex hormones affect B- and T-cell function. Lesions localized in the anterior basal hypothalamus depress delayed hypersensitivity reactions. On the other hand, the thymus exerts an effect on other endocrine glands. In the experimental animal, the immune response is accompanied by a fourfold increase in corticosterone levels and by a significant but small rise in thyroxine levels. Since the glucocorticoids are immunosuppressive, this reaction may form a modulating feedback loop.

Evidence for a role for the immune system in aging is more convincing for the diseases of old age than for the normal process of aging. However, the theory that normal aging is the consequence of a developing immunodeficiency is attractive, since the process is potentially accessible to manipulation. Restriction of calories delays maturation of the immune system and also delays the decline in function. Administration of lymphoid tissue that is rich in mature T-cells can extend threefold the life span of hypopituitary dwarf mice that are deficient in T-cells. Fractions of the thymic hormone(s) can serve as "replacement therapy" for the involuted thymus. Valid though these two descriptions of the aging process may be, they are still superficial. Man is a complex machine that relies on the fundamental capabilities of the cell to perform metabolic exchanges of material, to synthesize specific large molecules, and to reproduce. Within the nuclear material of the cell is the information that guides these activities. It is appropriate, therefore, to attempt to unravel the process of man's aging by studying aging in cells.

## Cellular Aspects of Aging

In considering the cellular aspects of aging, it is important to recall that the body contains several varieties of cells. First are cells that continue to divide throughout life, such as the basal cells of the epithelial surface of the body and the hemocytoblasts. These are referred to as *vegetative intermitotic* cells. Second are cells that continue to divide but differentiate at successive steps—*differentiating intermitotic* cells. Examples are the erythroblast and the spermatocyte. A third type is cells that are highly differentiated and normally do not undergo mitosis but may nevertheless be stimulated to divide when the need arises. This type of *postmitotic* cell is subclassified as *reverting*; an example is the hepatocyte. Finally there are cells such as neurons and myocardial cells that are *fixed* in their *postmitotic* state and incapable of division. Life of the individual intermitotic cell is terminated by cell division; that of the postmitotic cell by senescence and cell death. Postmitotic cells vary widely in their life span; most neurons survive for the whole life span of the individual, whereas at the other end of the scale, the fully differentiated epithelial cells of the alimentary mucosa survive no longer than a few days.

Because of these profound differences among cells, it is possible to give only general descriptions of the signs of senescence in cells. In general, in the aging cell the nucleus shows a clumping of chromatin, there is an increase in the number of nucleoli, and the nuclear membrane becomes invaginated. There is a reduction in the amount of rough endoplasmic reticulum, presumably concomitant with the lower synthetic activity of the aging cell. Changes have also been reported in the number and size of mitochondria, but the direction of change differs from tissue to tissue. More subtle changes in the mitochondria affect the pattern of the cristae. Typical of aging cells is the appearance of the chemically complex autofluorescent pigment lipofuscin. The pigment may be present in young cells, but the amount increases progressively with time and the accumulation may be large enough to displace the nucleus. Although this pigment accumulation is a general phenomenon, there are differences among tissues. In skeletal muscle, for example, more lipofuscin is deposited in the muscles of the limbs than in the muscles of the trunk; in the adrenal cortex, there is a preferential accumulation in the zona reticularis. The pigment granules are possibly lysosomes engorged with fragments of membrane, degenerated mitochondria, and other organelles. At the ultrastructural level, the pigment displays a banded structure sometimes associated with crystalline material. Old pigment granules may also contain vacuoles. Although the chemical structure has not been defined, there is evidence that there are several, perhaps tissue-specific, varieties of lipofuscin. Although lipofuscin has generally been regarded as inert, it may nonetheless have a functional role. The concept of the accumulation of intracellular inert material gave rise at one time to the "clinker" theory of cellular aging, in which the progressive occlusion of more and more of the cytoplasmic volume was the major metabolic depressant of the cell. In the experimental animal, lipofuscin accumulation has been shown to be accelerated by a deficiency of the antioxidant vitamin E. This raises the possibility that the pigment is the product of oxidative damage produced by free radicals.

## The Study of Cellular Aging

Two major experimental models exist for the study of aging at the cellular level. One involves serial transplantation of tissues, such as the mammary gland, into isogeneric animals. Experiments of this type have demonstrated that the transplanted tissue may outlive by several times the original donor animal. Aging of a tissue may thus be more the consequence of the cellular environment than an inherent cellular property. The second approach to the longitudinal study of cellular aging involves the in vitro culture of intermitotic cells. The early studies of Alexis Carrel led to the belief that cells in culture were essentially immortal, but recent work has suggested that the periodic replacement of the culture medium in his experiments introduced new young cells to the population.

Work by Hayflick and his associates (1979) with human fibroblasts in culture has shown that diploid cells are capable of only a limited number of divisions before they enter a phase of extended and irregular cycles and finally die. Fibroblasts taken from a fetal (or young) donor go through an average of 50 doublings of cell number. Cultures from older donors have a reduced number, but there is a very poor correlation between donor age and the number of cell divisions. Cells taken from young individuals who suffer from progeria or other syndrome(s) of "premature aging" show a subnormal doubling capability. These fibroblast cultures also show an increase in latency—the period between the establishment of the culture and the outgrowth of daughter cells—with increasing age. The aging fibroblast cells become large and less motile and accumulate glycogen, lipids, and lysosomes; there is irregularity and prolongation of the prereplicative phases of the cell cycle. Cells may be rescued from senescence by transformation from the diploid character into a neoplastic cell line; in this condition, the cells appear to have an infinite capacity to proliferate. Transplanted into an animal host, such cells are commonly malignant.

The growth of a human fibroblast culture in the early phase of rapid doubling can be interrupted by cooling. Upon rewarming, the culture begins to double again; the process starts at the point in the doublings count where the interruption occurred, even though the imposed dormancy might have lasted for years. The sum of the doublings before and after the interruption is characteristic of that particular culture. This evidence suggests that under these conditions, the aging and death of the cell are a programmed sequence brought about by specific aging genes. This is supported by evidence from cell fusion experiments in which "old" nuclei are transferred to "young" cytoplasts, or vice versa. In these transfers, the nucleus is dominant; however, a senescent nucleus is recessive when fused with the cytoplast of a neoplastic cell line.

There is recent tissue culture evidence that the enzyme 5'-nucleotidase increases in concentration with each cell doubling, and the level may increase tenfold by the time the cells are senescent. No such increase in concentration was found in transformed cells that were capable of an unlimited life span in vitro. Measurements of 5'-nucleotidase concentration in bone have yielded much higher values in the adult than in the neonate. It is postulated that increased levels of this enzyme might limit the availability of nucleotides for cell proliferation. The enzyme is responsible for the hydrolysis of adenosine monophosphate (AMP) and guanine monophosphate (GMP), and its increased concentration tends to prevent the reconversion of AMP to adenosine triphosphate (ATP) and thereby interferes with the energetics of the cell. There is also a link with an independent line of evidence concerning the role of nucleotides in cellular aging. In spleen cells of mice and in human

T-lymphocytes, the levels of cyclic AMP fall with increasing age while the levels of cyclic GMP rise. A similar change in the cAMP:cGMP ratio occurs in young individuals who have Down's syndrome, which produces some signs of accelerated aging. Furthermore, antagonistic actions of these two cyclic nucleotides are known to be involved in regulatory actions at the cellular level, so that changes in their ratio may be a factor in functional decline.

These tissue culture experiments, while clearly pointing to a programmed and limited life span in the cultured cell, may have little bearing on the process of aging in vivo where the cellular environment not only is more complex but is also somewhat more plastic than the rigidly controlled culture medium.

## Theories of Aging

Theories of the cellular basis of aging are current and may be grouped as (1) programmed aging, (2) errors arising in or damage to the cellular information system's DNA and RNA by environmental factors, and (3) depression of the cellular synthetic and metabolic activity of the cell by a humoral factor. These theories are described below.

### Cellular Aging as a Programmed Phenomenon

During embryonic development, tissues and organs undergo extensive and continuous remodeling. This is brought about by the orderly death of some cells and the activation of other lines controlled by genetic means. It is proposed that all cells, except germ cells and transformed cells, bear specific "death" genes programmed to switch off some cellular processes in a sequential fashion to produce in the tissue the aggregate sign of aging. In this way, cellular aging and death are the ends of cellular differentiation.

### The Error Theory

This theory is also based on the genetic information systems of the cell, DNA and RNA. It is proposed that the conversion of the information borne by these molecules into enzyme and protein synthesis becomes increasingly subject to error, thus leading to the accumulation of inappropriate molecules that are unable to support the cell's metabolism. This theory has been invoked as the mechanism underlying the fact that the life span of a species is inversely correlated with the rate of metabolism. The faster the rate of metabolism, the faster the rate of material turnover and the greater the chance for biochemical error.

### Repair Failure

Errors in the transcription of DNA, such as may be caused by experimental irradiation of the cell or by in vivo production of free radicals, can be corrected by repair processes. Two lines of evidence support the notion that aging is rooted in this mechanism: (1) the rate of DNA repair is related to the life span of the species, and (2) in cultured human cells, the rate of repair decreases as the cells age. The consequence, therefore, would again be the production of inappropriate molecules that are unable to support cell metabolism.

### Redundancy Failure

The genetic message borne by the DNA molecule has a high degree of redundancy; less than 1% of the information carried by the DNA is used by the cell, and gene sequences are repeated many times along the molecule. This theory supposes that as errors occur in gene synthesis, a supply of correct genes is available to take over from the ones damaged by error. As the cell ages, the supply of redundant genes becomes exhausted and the errors are then free to express themselves.

### The "Killer Hormone"

Denckla (1975) has proposed an alternative to these cellular theories that invokes a hormone derived from the pituitary gland that depresses the responsiveness of peripheral cells to the thyroid hormone. Two systems for which adequate thyroid activity appears to be necessary are the immune and the cardiovascular systems. Depression of the peripheral effects of the thyroid hormone by the pituitary factor may produce the decline and ultimate failure of these two major systems. This putative killer hormone appears to begin to be secreted at puberty, at which time it may buffer the tissues against the endocrine surge that occurs and it may restrain what otherwise would be an excessive metabolic response and burnout. Starvation, which when started before puberty delays it, extends the life span and also delays the appearance of this factor.

## Free Radicals and Aging

A unitary approach to the problem of aging has been advanced by Harman (1968). His theory proposes free radicals as a central agent in the changes seen with aging at the tissue, cellular, and subcellular levels. Free radicals are chemical intermediates that contain an unpaired electron. These molecules are highly reactive and commonly have a brief half-life. Free radicals occur normally in metabolic reactions—for example, in reactions involving chains of enzymes. In the visual system, free radicals are involved in the transduction of light energy to the electric signal. The free radicals involved in normal metabolic processes form part of a structured system and are not free to diffuse within the cell. Diffusible free radicals can produce deleterious effects. They may be formed from materials in the diet or in the atmosphere, or they may be formed by irradiation with ultraviolet light. The important adverse reactions of these radicals are (1) destruction of thiol groups with effects on thiol-dependent enzymes, and (2) lipid peroxidation with effects on biologic membranes of mitochondria, lysosomes, and the plasma membrane. Lipid peroxidation leads to the production of malonaldehyde, which reacts with protein to produce cross-links both within and between molecules. Malonaldehyde also reacts with DNA, where it leads to the liberation of free bases from the nucleotides.

Usually these effects express themselves as impaired information transfer in the cell, loss of specific membrane functions, impaired enzyme activity, formation of the membrane-based "aging pigment," and the cross-linking typical of aging collagen and elastin as well as reorganization of the mucopolysaccharides of connective tissue ground substance.

A major attraction of this theory is that free radical peroxidation can be prevented by antioxidants, both natural and artificial. Proponents of this theory, therefore, regard the aging process as treatable. Vitamin E and vitamin C are significant natural antioxidants, and the toluene derivative butylated hydroxy toluene (BHT) is an antioxidant commonly used as a food additive. Although the possibility that peroxidation is fundamental to aging has been extensively investigated, the evidence has at best been equivocal. Some animal experiments have extended the life span by incorporating an antioxidant into the diet. A Rumanian study, which has not been successfully repeated, showed some improved survival of elderly individuals who took vitamin E. Other experiments have suggested that antioxidants are effective only when the conditions of the experiment tend to shorten the life span of control animals. Still other studies have shown no effect on the rate of aging or on the life span.

A number of proposals have been made as alternatives to the central role of antioxidants in retarding cellular aging in an attempt to explain observations in which the life span of treated animals was increased. Some of the proposed mechanisms are the following:

1. Antioxidants depress appetite, reduce food intake, and thus delay growth and maturation and lengthen life span.
2. Antioxidants suppress tumor growth, which is commonly the cause of death in longevity studies.
3. Antioxidants retard the aging decline of immune processes.

Clearly, it is not possible to identify among this spectrum of theories one that is overwhelmingly supported by the evidence. It may well be that the predominant aging process differs from one person to another and that the cellular and subcellular changes that occur can operate in a variety of combinations to produce the common result of functional impairment.

## SUGGESTED READING

Burnet F.M.: An immunological approach to aging. *Lancet* 2:358, 1970.
Denckla W.D.: A time to die. *Life Sci.* 16:31–44, 1975.
Goldstein A.L., Thurman G.B., Low T.L.K., et al.: Thymosin: The endocrine thymus and its role in the aging process, in Cherkin A., et al. (eds.): *Physiology and Cell Biology of Aging*. New York, Raven Press, 1979, pp. 51–60.
Harman D.: Free radical theory of aging: Effect of free radical inhibitors on the mortality rate of LAF$_1$ mice. *Gerontology* 23:476, 1968.
Hayflick L.: Cell aging, in Cherkin A., et al. (eds.): *Physiology and Cell Biology of Aging*. New York, Raven Press, 1979, pp. 3–19.
Morrow J., Garner C.: An evaluation of some theories of the mechanism of aging. *Gerontology* 25:136–144, 1979.
Strehler B.L.: Aging at the cellular level, Rossman I. (eds.): in *Clinical Geriatrics*. Philadelphia, J.B. Lippincott Co., 1971, pp. 49–87.
Sun A.S., Aggarwal B.B., Packer L.: Enzyme levels of normal human cells: Aging in culture. *Arch. Biochem. Biophys.* 170:1, 1975.
Walford R.L.: Immunological theory of aging: Current status. *Fed. Proc.* 33:2020, 1974.

# 3 / Aging Changes in Body Conformation and Composition

ALTHOUGH THE FUNDAMENTAL PROCESS of aging occurs at the cellular level, it is expressed not only in changed function but also in a changed anatomy of the body. Major signs of aging are seen in both the conformation and the composition of the body.

## Body Conformation

Most measurement studies have been of the cross-sectional type. As we have seen, such studies are likely to be misleading because of secular changes—for example, those that have occurred in stature over the years. Such cross-sectional studies have revealed an apparent loss of height with aging, which begins at 30 years of age and progresses at a rate of 1 cm per decade thereafter. Longitudinal studies and remeasurement studies involving a shorter time span show a variability in the age of onset of the loss of height and a rate of loss only about half that suggested by cross-sectional studies. Some studies, for example, have shown an increase in height extending into the 40s before any decline begins. This "late growth" has been attributed to the development of a more erect posture and to some continued growth of the vertebrae. Measurements of sitting height suggest that the loss of stature is divided almost equally between trunk length and length of the extremities. Shrinkage, however, does not begin at the same time in the two components; some loss of leg length precedes loss of trunk length. Measurements of the length of the femur show almost no age-related change, and a significant part of the loss of standing height must be produced by changes in the joints and by a flattening of the arch of the foot. An increase in the spinal curvature and some compaction of the intervertebral disks contribute to the loss of trunk length. There is only a slight reduction in arm span with age, which tends to validate, to some extent, the notion that the height attained at maturity can be estimated from the span when shrinkage of stature has already occurred.

21

Shoulder width decreases with age in both sexes, in part due to loss of muscle mass in the deltoids. In both sexes, the pelvic diameter increases. Changes in the elasticity of the lungs and thorax lead to an increase in chest circumference with age. The increase occurs first in the anterior-posterior diameter; the lateral diameter may decrease in the very old. The depth of the abdomen measured with the person in the supine position increases steadily from young adulthood onward; the increase averages about 3 cm between the ages of 25 and 70. The circumference of the head shrinks slightly up to age 60; thereafter, it has been reported to return to the young adult value, presumably as a result of continued laying down of bone. The nose and ears continue to grow in length beyond maturity; the nose also becomes broader and the ear lobes thicken.

In men, body weight tends to increase to the middle 50s and thereafter to decline. The rate of weight loss accelerates in the late 60s and 70s. In women, body weight continues to increase into the 60s and then to decline, but at a rate slower than that in men. The increase in body weight in middle age (the "middle-age spread") appears to be the product of reduced physical activity in an environment where food is plentiful, since members of more primitive societies do not show this change.

## Body Composition

The gross composition of the body may be studied by several noninvasive means. Measurement of *total body water* by an indicator dilution method provides an index of the adiposity of the body, since fat contains very little intracellular or extracellular water. Another approach to determining adiposity depends on the fact that fat is the only component of the body that is lighter than water. Measurement of *specific gravity,* by weighing an individual in air and in water, provides a moderately reliable index of the relative contribution of adipose tissue to body weight. Assessment of the amount of subcutaneous fat is made by measuring the *skin-fold thickness* at selected sites. Measurements of adiposity by one of these means lead to the concept of *fat-free mass* or *lean body mass*. The former measures all the fat-free substances of the body, whereas the latter includes the structural lipid substances.

An alternative concept is the *body cell mass*, which is defined as the mass that uses oxygen; it includes muscle and the parenchymal cells but excludes the dense supporting tissues such as bone and cartilage. Since cells typically have a high potassium content while the extracellular material contains very little, body cell mass may be estimated from the size of the pool of exchangeable potassium measured using dilution of the isotope $^{42}$K. Since some part of the pool of body potassium exchanges only very slowly, or in fact is nonaccessible, a preferred measurement involves whole body counting of the naturally occurring $^{40}$K.

At any age, there is a wide variation among individuals in body weight, the fraction contributed by fat, and the total volume of body water (Fig 3–1). In an "average" young man (one neither strikingly lean nor obviously obese), the total body water measured as the volume of distribution of antipyrine or deuterium oxide is 60% of the body weight; in a young woman, the value is less—approximately 52%. With aging, the value declines to approximately 54% in the man and 46% in the woman. That this alteration is brought about by a change in the ratio of lean to fat rather than by a general dehydration of the tissues is demonstrated by a de-

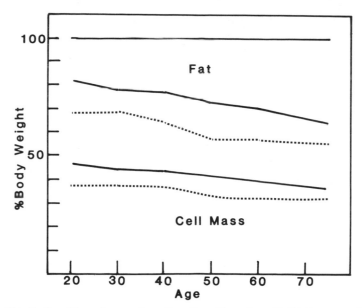

**Fig 3–1.**—The change in adiposity with aging. Solid lines are the values for men; dotted lines are the values for women. (Based on data from Novak L.P.J.: *Gerontology* 27:438, 1972.)

crease in the specific gravity of the body. The typical value of 1.08 in the 30-year-old man falls to 1.03 at age 70. This change in specific gravity is more striking in the man than in the woman because men are more lean initially.

The change in skin-fold thickness with age depends very much on the site of the measurement. The thickness of the fold on the dorsum of the hand or over the triceps decreases from the age of 50 onward in men as does the thickness of the humeral and scapular folds. Paraumbilical thickness increases until the 70s before showing any decline. In women, most skin-fold measurements tend to remain constant until the age of 65 except at the scapular, mammary, and chin sites, which increase in thickness into the 70s. One must conclude that the greater part of the extra adipose tissue in the aged is laid down internally, within organs, in the mesentery or perinephric areas rather than in subcutaneous sites.

The two major divisions of body water, intracellular and extracellular fluids, do not diminish equally with age (Fig 3–2). In the young adult, the volumes of these components have a ratio of 2:1. The reduction in fluid volume that occurs with age is more marked in the intracellular than in the extracellular spaces, so that the ratio

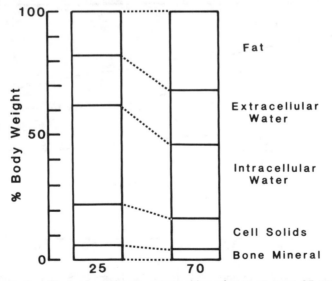

**Fig 3–2.**—Typical proximate composition of men at ages 25 and 70. Note especially the changing ratio of intracellular and extracellular water.

becomes less than 2:1, tending toward the values seen in the pre-adolescent. This change could reflect either a dehydration of the cells or a loss of cell mass with maintained hydration.

Estimates of the cell mass of the body made either by measuring exchangeable potassium or by the preferred procedure of whole body counting of $^{40}K$ reveal a reduction of cell mass relative to body weight. In men, total body potassium decreases from a value of 54 mEq/kg body weight at age 40 to 40 to 50 mEq/kg at age 70. There is a similar percent change in women, but absolute values are lower by approximately 8 mEq/kg body weight.

Although most of the loss of lean body mass occurs in muscle, virtually all organs participate in this age-related loss of mass, though to varying degrees. On the one hand, the lungs show no loss of weight or, in fact, may show an increase; on the other, the liver and kidneys lose a third of their weight between ages 30 and 90. An exception to this pattern of loss is the prostate, which doubles in weight between youth and old age.

Just as potassium can be used as a marker of the intracellular space, exchangeable sodium ($Na^+_e$) can be used as a marker of the extracellular. Between ages 30 and 60, the ratio $Na_e:K_e$ rises from 1.0:1 to 1.2:1 (Figs 3–3 and 3–4). These studies are in agreement

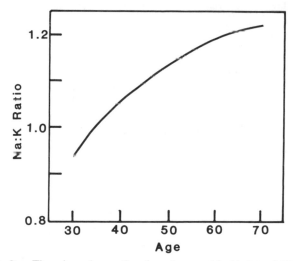

**Fig 3–3.**—The changing ratio of exchangeable $Na^+$ and $K^+$. (Based on data from MacGillivray I., Buchanan T.J., Billewicz W.Z.: *Clin. Sci.* 19:17–25, 1960.)

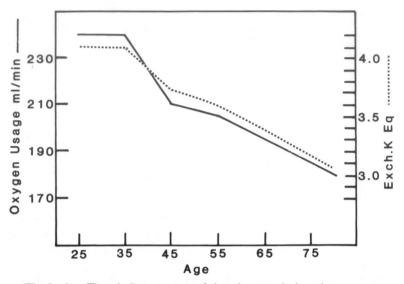

**Fig 3–4.**—The similar courses of the changes in basal oxygen consumption and in exchangeable K⁺ content.

with direct analysis of muscle and visceral tissues in demonstrating a shift in favor of extracellular components with aging. Most studies of man in this area have been of the cross-sectional type, but the relatively few remeasurement studies have produced essentially the same picture.

In summary, with increasing age there are a small loss of height, a modest loss of weight, a small consequent loss of body surface area, and a significant loss of active cell mass. In the old, the body is housing a smaller engine. It is important to keep this in mind when considering the decline of function with age. Common measurements of function such as metabolic rate, the rate of glomerular filtration or perfusion of the kidney, and cardiac output are all standardized for comparison of one individual with another or for comparison with a normal value for a given surface area. This places the old individual at a disadvantage and may obscure the fact that a reduced function might be appropriate for the decreased tissue mass it serves. For example, the resting rate of oxygen consumption declines significantly between ages 30 and 70, but this decline does not appear when the rate of use is standardized to cell mass as estimated by the amount of exchangeable potassium.

Acknowledgement of the altered composition of the body in the old is also vital for the appropriate use of drugs in treating this group.

## SUGGESTED READING

Boddy K., King P.C., Womersley J., et al.: Body potassium and fat-free mass. *Clin. Sci.* 44:622–625, 1973.

Damon A., Seltzer C.C., Stoudt H.W., et al.: Age and physique in healthy white veterans at Boston. *Aging Hum. Dev.* 3:202–208, 1972.

Durnin J.V.G.A., Womersley J.: Body fat assessed from total body density and its estimation from skin fold thickness: Measurements on 481 men and women aged from 16 to 72 years. *Br. J. Nutr.* 32:77–79, 1974.

Fryer J.H.: Studies of body composition in men aged 60 and over, in Shock N.W. (ed.): *Biological Aspects of Aging.* New York, Columbia Press, 1962, pp. 59–78.

Hooton E.A., Dupertuis C.W.: Age changes and selective survival in Irish males. *Stud. Phys. Anthropol.* 2:1–130, 1951.

Lye M.: Distribution of body potassium in healthy elderly subjects. *Gerontology* 27:286–292, 1981.

MacGillivray I., Buchanan T.J., Billewicz W.Z.: Values for total exchangeable sodium and potassium in normal females based on weight, height and age. *Clin. Sci.* 19:17–25, 1960.

Miall W.E., Ashcroft M.T., Lovell H.G., et al.: A longitudinal study of the decline of adult height with age in two Welsh communities. *Hum. Biol.* 39:445–454, 1967.

Moore F., Olesen K.H., McMurrey J.D., et al.: *The Body Cell Mass and Its Supporting Environment.* Philadelphia, W.B. Saunders Co., 1963.

Novak L.P.: Aging, total body potassium, fat free mass and cell mass in males and females between ages 18 and 85 years. *Gerontology* 27:438–443, 1972.

Pett L.B., Ogilvie G.F.: The Canadian weight-height survey. *Hum. Biol.* 28:177–188, 1956.

Rossman I.: Anatomic and body composition changes with aging, Finch C.E., Hayflick L. (eds.): *Handbook of the Biology of Aging.* New York, Van Nostrand Reinhold Co., 1977.

# PART II

# AGING OF TISSUES AND ORGAN SYSTEMS

# 4 / Blood, Supporting Tissues, Muscle, Skin, and Teeth

## Blood

The red blood cells show morphological and biochemical changes as they age, which ultimately results in their removal from the circulation after a life span of 120 days. Aging cells lose potassium, become increasingly dense, and are increasingly fragile to mechanical or osmotic challenge. The red blood cells of old individuals show only subtle differences from those of young persons. There is a small increase in mean cell diameter and mean corpuscular volume and also an increase in fragility measured in terms of the tonicity that produces 50% hemolysis. In old persons, there is also an increased variability of the cell fragility. This age-related change may be due to a change in the relationship of volume to surface area in the average cell or it may reflect a decrease in the efficiency of the spleen and lymphoid tissue to remove aged cells. Estimations of the life span of red blood cells, however, show this to be essentially the same as in the young.

The blood volume is well maintained in persons until they reach approximately 80 years of age, so up to this time the ratio of blood volume to active tissue mass increases. In healthy individuals, the red blood cell count, hematocrit value, and hemoglobin concentration remain within the normal range to age 65; thereafter, there may be a slight decrease. It seems likely that a major cause of the relatively high incidence of anemia in old individuals reported in hospital surveys is chronic disease, with some contribution from suboptimal nutrition as a result of poverty, lack of mobility, or decreased interest in food. The erythrocyte sedimentation rate is increased in the old, probably as a result of changes in the plasma protein concentrations, especially that of fibrinogen. A small increase in viscosity is seen in older men, perhaps again due to the increased fibrinogen concentration.

Few significant morphological changes occur in the white blood cells. Granulocytes show increased lobulation and reduced granulation; their osmotic resistance increases. Lymphocyte production is reduced, but there is an increased concentration of RNA in the cell.

Platelet count and function remain unchanged.

Plasma protein concentrations decrease with age, due mainly to a reduction in the albumin fraction. There is a small rise in the globulin fraction. As a consequence, the albumin/globulin ratio falls and the colloid osmotic pressure is reduced. The fibrinogen concentration rises by approximately 25% between ages 30 and 70. This appears to be the only change in the clotting factors. The amount of low density lipoprotein increases with age, more in women than in men; the amount of high density lipoprotein shows only a minor change in both sexes. Although these changes in plasma protein may be directly related to aging, similar alterations can occur with hypoactivity.

There is no age-related change in plasma osmotic pressure and only minor alterations in the chemical composition of the plasma. The level of ionized calcium shows a slight decrease; the plasma bicarbonate level falls at a rate of approximately 1% per decade from age 50 onward. Since the arterial blood $PCO_2$ remains stable in the absence of respiratory dysfunction, the pH falls from the young adult value of 7.40 to 7.38 in old age. The plasma concentrations of nitrogenous metabolites, urea, uric acid, and creatinine rise as renal function declines with age.

The amount of active red bone marrow diminishes with age, being replaced by yellow marrow. The loss occurs first in the long bones and more slowly in the flat bones, and there is very little reduction in the level of vertebral red bone marrow. The cytology of the remaining red marrow is the same as in the young.

The functional reserve for hemopoiesis—that is, the ability to accelerate the production of red blood cells and to convert yellow bone marrow to the red, cell-producing variety when challenged by a need to replace lost cells—is reduced in the elderly, but in practice the response to hemorrhage, although impaired, remains adequate.

## Supporting Tissues

With aging, there is a relative increase in the size of the extracellular component of body water. This water is distributed among the solid and semisolid components of the extracellular material, which make up the supporting tissues of the body, the connective tissue, cartilage, and bone. These tissues are characterized by the very high proportion of material that is extracellular.

## Connective Tissues

Throughout life, the supporting matrix changes. In the infant, it is a highly aqueous environment for the cells. As the tissue matures, there is a decrease in the amount of water and an increase in the solid components. Typically, these solid materials are polymers that are more condensed as the tissue ages. Connective tissue has two major components: ground substance, which consists of mucopolysaccharides in the form of a hydrated gel, and fibrous proteins, collagen, elastin, and reticular fibers. These substances are synthesized by fibroblasts.

Ground substance differs from one location to another depending on the function that needs to be served. In tissues that require mobility, the major component is hyaluronic acid; in tissues that need mechanical support and firmness, chondroitin sulfate is found.

Intermediate between ground substance and the fibrous elements of connective tissue is basement membrane, which consists of glycoprotein organized in a fine fibrillary form. The basement membrane defines the boundary between epithelial or endothelial tissues and connective tissue. It is thus a barrier that must be crossed twice by material in transit between blood and cell.

The age-related changes in ground substance are essentially part of the process of maturation, with an increase in the density of the gel and a loss of water. The volume occupied by ground substance is reduced as the fiber density increases.

Diffusion of material within the extracellular component is potentially impaired with age and cell mobility is reduced. These changes threaten both the nutrition of cells and the repair and healing processes.

Collagen is formed by the aggregation of molecules of tropocollagen. The aggregation occurs both end to end and side to side. The molecules of tropocollagen are staggered in the side-by-side relationship by one quarter of the long dimension. This produces the characteristic cross-banding of the collagen fibers at the periodicity of 6,400 A. As the tissue matures and ages, collagen fibers increase in number and in size. Cross-linkage develops between fibers. The solubility of the collagen is reduced, and the structure becomes more stable. This reduced rate of turnover is evidenced by reduced excretion in the aged of hydroxyproline, the marker amino acid of collagen. The mechanical properties of the fibers change; greater force is required to produce a given degree of extension and, once stretched, the fibers only slowly return to their original length (hysteresis).

In extreme old age, there is an increase in the concentration of the enzyme collagenase. The phase of increasing rigidity of the tissue matrix is thus followed by a phase of weakening.

Fibers of elastin also develop cross-linkages as they age; water is lost and the fibers become more intensely yellow. The fibers become more rigid and under continued stress tend to fray and fragment. In some cases, the lost elastic fibers are replaced by collagen.

The delicate reticular fibers of the connective tissue are abundant in the young but with maturation of the tissue are replaced by fibers of collagen.

Aging is also associated with the appearance of a fourth fiber element, pseudo-elastin. Chemically it is intermediate in composition between collagen and elastin. Structurally it appears to consist of collagen with a coat of amorphous material, which masks the typical cross-banding of collagen.

Hyaline cartilage dehydrates as it ages and is converted to fibrocartilage. The articular cartilage, which in the young person is translucent, becomes opaque and yellow with age; elasticity is lost and the cartilage thins in weight-bearing areas—for example, the menisci of the knee joint. In both connective tissue and cartilage, the increasing fiber density provides nidi for the deposition of bone mineral. Calcification occurs in the major blood vessels; cartilage may be converted to true bone.

The effects of the aging changes in the connective tissue are global. Skin loses its elasticity and wrinkles, joints become stiffened by the increase in fibrous tissue around them, lungs lose their elastic recoil, and costal cartilages become increasingly rigid. Loss of hydration in the nucleus pulposus of the intervertebral disks leads to compaction of the vertebrae and shrinkage in stature. The cardiovascular system, which depends to a great extent on the properties of distensibility and elasticity, is greatly impaired as the matrix changes. The chambers of the heart become less distensible and as a consequence there is less contractility; the elastic arteries become more rigid and lose their "windkessel" function; valves stiffen and even the pacemaker cells of the nodal tissue may be displaced by collagen fibers.

## Bone

Although the tendency in the fibrous tissues is for calcium to be deposited, bone loses mineral as it ages. The development of this osteoporosis involves a loss of as much as 10% of the bone salts. In the long bones, the net loss of mineral is associated with remodeling. The bone erodes from within, while deposition is occurring at a slower rate at the periosteal surface. The external diameter of the bone increases and the wall becomes thinner. Haversian canals enlarge, and the space that develops in the bone becomes filled with adipose and fibrous tissue. The thinning of the cortex of the long bones weakens them and fractures occur under even slight loads.

The loss of bone mass is unequal between the sexes. At age 20, bone mass is greater in women than in men. The bone loss that begins in young adulthood is more rapid in women, so that by age 50, bone mass is equal in the two sexes. After menopause, bone loss accelerates in women and the incidence of osteoporosis is several times higher than in men. A woman aged 80 has one chance in five of sustaining a fracture of the neck of the femur.

Many factors are involved in this process of mineral depletion, and the following explanations have been offered:

1. After growth and modeling of bone are completed in the young adult, an imbalance of osteoclastic and osteoblastic activity develops. This imbalance is exacerbated by the sudden withdrawal of estrogen during the menopause.

2. Calcitonin secretion is modified by the level of circulating estrogen. As estrogen levels fall, the balance between parathormone and calcitonin shifts in favor of parathormone, which affects bone directly and increases the renal excretion of mineral.

3. There is an age-related decrease in the circulating level of hydroxylated vitamin $D_3$, which impairs intestinal absorption of calcium and causes an increasing reliance on bone for the maintenance of adequate calcium levels.

## Muscle

Characteristic of the aging process is a loss of muscle mass, which may amount to a 30% loss between ages 30 and 80. Muscle cells also show the general signs of cellular aging: the accumulation of lipofuscin and an increase in the lipid content. The loss of muscle mass is due to a reduction in both the number and the size of muscle fibers. Sarcomeres are lost from the fibers, thereby reducing the effective length. The consequences of this are a limitation of the tension that can be developed at a particular muscle length and a reduction in the range of movement that can be produced by contraction. The reduction in the number of fibers is greater in red muscle than in white. In the senescent rat, it has been shown that the reduction in mass correlates well with a decrease in the number of myofibrils. Changes can be seen in the sarcolemma, and the T-tubule system proliferates. In the periphery of the muscle fibers, there is evidence of continuing protein synthesis, but the product does not become organized and presumably represents an abortive attempt at regeneration. In agreement with the general principle of tissue aging that there is an increase in the extracellular components, the aging muscle shows an increase in connective tissue. The muscle spindles are somewhat reduced in diameter, but there is no change in number.

There is an age-related loss of motoneurons, but their number is reduced less than that of muscle fibers. As a consequence, the size of the motor units is reduced. For a muscle to work against a particular load, therefore, an increased number of motor units must be recruited, and the individual perceives this as an increase in effort.

At the motor end plate, an unfolding of the membrane and a reduction of the area occupied by the junction occur. The aging muscle shows an absolute fall in the content of ATP, a decrease in the ATP:ADP ratio, and a fall in the content of both glycogen and creatine phosphate.

There is no change in the resting membrane potential of aging muscle, but there is a reduction in the frequency of miniature end plate potentials—i.e., a reduction in the spontaneous release of quanta of neurotransmitter. This may reflect reduced synthesis and axonal transport in the motor nerves. In the old individual, the electromyogram typically shows a decrease in amplitude, a prolongation of the individual action potentials, and an increase in the number of polyphasic potentials. There is also evidence of an increase in both absolute and relative refractory periods in senescent muscle. The latent period, contraction period, and relaxation period are lengthened, and the rate of development of peak tension is reduced.

Changes in the overall muscle strength begin at approximately age 35, but the degree of loss differs widely among muscle groups. Moreover, the assessment of muscle strength in the old individual is likely to be confused by changes in motivation, joint stiffness, and the ability of the muscle to obtain adequate oxygenation. Changes of senescence are significantly less in muscles in which activity is maintained.

### Skin and Appendages

Skin serves a number of vital functions. It is a major receptor site for collecting information at the interface between the body and the environment, it is a rather impermeable barrier preventing loss of water from the body, it is a barrier against invasion by microorganisms, and by virtue of its high vascularity, it acts as the major organ of thermoregulation. The skin consists of two parts: the surface epithelial layer and the underlying corium. In the young person, the basal surface of the epithelium is undulant, forming "pegs" that project downward into the corium. As the skin ages, the pegs disappear and the basal layer becomes flattened. As a consequence, the area of the stratum germinativum is reduced and the number of germinal cells decreases. Both eccrine sweat glands and sebaceous glands are lost, and as a consequence, the skin tends to become dry and flaky. Melanophore activity declines, producing an aging pallor. The skin in the old appears thin and translucent; this thinning is mainly due to changes in the connective tissue. In the young person, the elastic properties of the subcutaneous tissues hold the skin bunched and taut. As elasticity is lost, the skin extends and falls into wrinkles and folds. Wrinkling affects the whole body surface but is most obvious in areas of heavy use, such as those overlying the facial muscles of expression.

Loss of subcutaneous adipose tissue in many parts of the body reduces the skin's effectiveness as a thermal insulator. The thinning and drying of the skin reduce the barrier functions, thus allowing easier access of microorganisms and an enhanced loss of water vapor from the deep tissue.

With aging, nail growth slows. Changes in the composition of the nail, mainly a deposition of calcium, produce a dull, yellow appearance; the lunula (half-moon) disappears and the nails develop longitudinal ridges. Thickening of the nails is more marked on the toes than the fingers, and toenails may become hooked or curved.

Hair loss is a common feature of aging, beginning in the 30s in most men and after menopause in women. Hair loss is not confined to the scalp but also affects axillary and pubic hair, where loss tends to occur from the periphery inward. In the very old, total loss of body hair is sometimes reported. Loss of the outer third of the eyebrows, which is a common sign of myxedema, occurs in many older euthyroid individuals. Old men may show an increased growth of hair on eyebrows, in the nostrils, and around the borders of the ears.

Graying of the axillary hair is a reliable sign of aging; in fact, the degree of graying correlates more precisely with age than almost any other anatomical or physiologic variable. Graying of the scalp hair is a less reliable sign, since hereditary factors play a greater role here. Graying commonly begins in the middle to late 30s in whites and significantly later in blacks.

### Teeth and Oral Structures

The state of the teeth at any particular time is more the result of dental hygiene than of age. At age 65, half the population have lost all their natural teeth to caries or periodontal disease and two-thirds have no teeth in one or the other jaw. Loss of teeth is more common in the maxilla than in the mandible. Although the teeth are exposed to constant abrasion, they are so durable that it has been suggested that under ideal conditions they should last for at least two life spans. Healthy, well-preserved teeth do, however, show some true signs of aging.

The major change observed in *enamel* is loss through attrition and the development of pigmentation in the superficial layers. Animal experiments have suggested that associated with the increased pigmentation is a decrease in the permeability (already very small) of the enamel. *Dentin* is a dynamic component of the teeth and its formation is stimulated by a number of factors, including wear, caries, and irritation. The dentin is also believed to be laid down as a normal aging process. There appears to be a cycling between odontoblasts and cells of the dental pulp, with odontoblasts degenerating or differentiating into pulp cells and cells from the pulp replacing the lost cells. The continued odontoblastic activity reduces the size of the pulp cavity. With aging, the dentin becomes more opaque and less hydrated and has an increased fluoride content.

Dental pulp diminishes in volume as its space is invaded by dentin, and by age 70, the pulp space of many teeth has been obliterated. The cell population of the pulp, mainly fibroblasts, decreases beginning in the early 20s. Age-related changes are also seen in the blood vessels and the nerve supply of the pulp, so there is a progressive reduction of both perfusion and sensitivity. The connective tissue of the pulp, which consists of ground substance, reticular fibers, and collagen, becomes more dense with dehydration of the ground substance and fibrosis. With the increasing density of fibers in the pulp areas of calcification, pulpstones appear.

The cement substance that invests the root of the tooth continues to be laid down throughout life. Although the rate of formation diminishes, the tooth is still attached to the periodontal tissues. The periodontal ligament, which serves as a suspensory sling for the tooth, is attached to the cement substance and the alveolar bone. With aging, the ligament is thinned and the fibers lose their alignment. This is probably the result of a reduction of the loading placed on the ligament as occlusal teeth are lost or a diet requiring less mastication is adopted and is not a real aging effect.

The gingiva or gum consists of two parts: the attached gingiva, which covers the alveolar bone, and the free gingiva, which forms a cuff around the enamel of the tooth. Since the free part of the gum is not attached, there is a potential space or cleft. The common change of aging is the recession of the gum away from the tooth, thus exposing the junction between enamel and cement substances and forming a pocket in which bacteria and food debris can lodge. The stratified epithelium of the gum thins and loses the degree of keratinization that is present in the young.

The alveolar bone participates in the general loss of bone mineral with age and the bone matrix is resorbed. This process of resorption accelerates when teeth are lost.

The epithelial lining of the mouth undergoes a slowing of cell proliferation, and the healing of abrasions is impaired. In addition, the surface becomes drier as a result of reduced mucin secretion coupled with a reduced flow from the salivary glands. The epithelial surface of the tongue becomes smooth as filiform papillae are lost. In the circumvalate papillae, taste buds atrophy and produce changes in gustatory sensation. An individual aged 70 has only 30% of the original complement of taste buds. Prosthetic replacement of teeth reduces taste sensation and fails to restore normal masticatory ability. In addition, a prosthesis robs the individual of texture sense, which contributes to the enjoyment of food. These factors influence a person's food selection. There is a tendency for the older individual to choose salty or very sweet foods that require little chewing.

## SUGGESTED READING

### BLOOD

Bowdler A.J., Dougherty R.M., Bowdler N.C.: Age as a factor affecting erythrocyte osmotic fragility in males. *Gerontology* 27:224–231, 1981.

Cerny L.C., Cook L.B., Valone F.: The erythrocyte in aging. *Exp. Gerontol.* 7:137–142, 1972.

Goldman R.: Decline in organ function with aging, Rossman I. (ed.): in *Clinical Geriatrics*. Philadelphia, J.B. Lippincott Co., 1979, p. 42.

Hyams D.E.: The blood, in Brocklehurst J.C. (ed.): *Textbook of Geriatric Medicine and Gastroenterology*. Edinburgh, Churchill Livingstone, Inc., 1973, pp. 528–532.

### SUPPORTING TISSUES

Beausoleil N., Sparrow D., Rowe J., et al.: Longitudinal analysis of the influence of age on bone loss in men. *Gerontologist* 20:63, 1980.

Ciara S.M.: Bone loss and aging, in Goldman R., Rockstein M. (eds.): *The Physiology and Pathology of Aging*. New York, Academic Press, 1975.

Exton-Smith A.N.: Bone aging and metabolic bone disease, in Brocklehurst J.C. (ed.): *Textbook of Geriatric Medicine and Gerontology*. Edinburgh, Churchill Livingstone, Inc., 1973, pp. 476–491.

Hall D.A.: Metabolic and structural aspects of aging, in Brocklehurst J. C. (ed.): *Textbook of Geriatric Medicine and Gerontology*. Edinburgh, Churchill Livingstone, Inc., 1973, pp. 21–32.

### MUSCLE

Gutman E.: Muscle, in Finch C.E., Hayflick L. (eds.): *Handbook of the Biology of Aging*. New York, Von Nostrand Reinhold Co. 1977.

Shephard R.J.: *Endurance Fitness*. Toronto, University of Toronto Press, 1977.

Shephard R.J.: *Physical Activity and Aging*. Chicago, Croon Helm, 1978.

Shock N.W., Norris A.H.: Neuromuscular coordination as a factor in age changes in muscular exercise, in Brumer D., Jokl E. (eds.): *Physical Activity and Aging*. Baltimore, University Park Press, 1970.

SKIN

Korting G.W.: *Geriatric Dermatology*, Curth W., Curth H.O. (trans.). Philadelphia, W.B. Saunders Co., 1980, pp. 3–8.

ORAL CAVITY

Zack L.: The oral cavity, in Rossman I. (ed.): *Clinical Geriatrics*. Philadelphia, J.B. Lippincott Co., 1979, pp. 618–637.

# 5 / The Respiratory System, the Cardiovascular System, and Physical Activity in Aging

MANY PEOPLE first appreciate the process of aging when they realize that everyday tasks require more effort than before and that they can sustain decreasing levels of physicial activity. This decline is early in its onset and insidious in its progress. A healthy 30-year-old, for example, would be hard pressed to match the sustained activity of a 10-year-old at play. Changes in the muscle and the supporting tissues contribute to this functional decline, but a major role is played by the person's decreased ability to acquire and deliver oxygen to the active tissues. Each step in the path oxygen takes from the air to the metabolizing cell is vulnerable to aging.

## Respiratory System

At age 20, a person has about $300 \times 10^6$ alveoli, providing an alveolar exchange surface of approximately 80 sq m. The number of alveoli remains virtually constant in the healthy aging individual, but the alveoli become smaller and more shallow, thus reducing the alveolar surface area to 65 to 70 sq m by age 70. The alveolar ducts appear to increase in size and this compresses the alveoli. The total lung volume remains virtually constant throughout life, but the vital capacity falls at a steady rate from young adulthood. Between ages 20 and 60, about 1 L of capacity is lost.

The position of the chest wall in the resting condition—that is, at the end of a quiet expiration—is determined by the balance achieved between two elastic forces. The lung is tending to collapse and the thoracic wall is tending to move outward. These forces communicate with each other via the fluid layer between the visceral and the parietal layers of pleura, which provides a negative (subatmospheric) pressure in the potential interpleural space. In the young person, the equilibrium between the lung and the chest wall is reached at a lung volume of approximately 50% of the total lung capacity. Active expiration, in which the muscles of the thorax and to some extent the diaphragm work against the chest wall elastic forces to compress the lung, can reduce the contained volume of air to approximately 20% of the total lung capacity (the residual volume). The air moved by such an expiration is the expiratory reserve volume. With aging, the lung loses elasticity, and therefore it requires less force to stretch it a unit amount; the lung becomes more compliant and the pressure-volume curve shifts to the left. Since there is a smaller force working against the elastic forces of the chest wall, the rib cage expands. In the older person, therefore, there is an increase in the functional residual capacity, which at age 60 is approximately 60% of the total lung capacity rather than the 50% characteristic of the young adult. This is shown as an increase in the anterior-posterior diameter of the thoracic cage (Fig 5–1).

Although it is well established that the "elastic recoil" of the lungs is reduced in the aged, this does not appear to be due to a

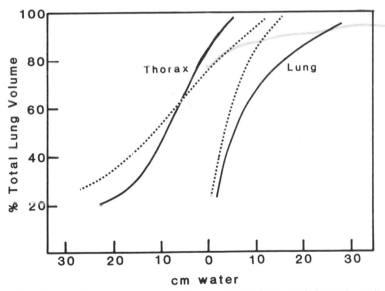

**Fig 5–1.**—The changing compliance of the lung and thoracic wall. Solid lines represent the 25-year-old; dotted lines the 70-year-old. (Based on data from Turner J.M., Mead J., Wohl M.E.J.: *Appl. Physiol.* 25:664–671, 1968.)

reduction in the amount of elastin in the lung; in fact, the amount of elastin increases. Collagen, by virtue of its helical arrangement around alveolar ducts and alveoli, contributes significantly to the elastic properties. The development of covalent cross-linkages between collagen fibers, which occurs rather generally in aging connective tissue, may reduce the springlike properties of the helices. A further important contribution to lung elasticity comes from the surface forces at the air-alveolar interface. The extent to which the surfactant changes with age is presently unknown.

Changes in the thoracic wall involving some calcification and stiffening of the cartilaginous articulations of the ribs together with changes in the spinal curvatures make the chest wall less compliant. On balance, the decreased compliance of the chest wall exceeds the increased compliance of the lung, and thus the total compliance of the system decreases. More muscular work is required, therefore, to move air in and out of the lung. In the old individual, the residual volume increases, and in spite of some increase in the functional residual capacity, the reserve volume available for forced expiration decreases. Typical young and old values of these lung volumes are shown in Figure 5–2. The diaphragm contributes significantly to changes in the thoracic volume, and this is exploited to an increased extent in older persons to minimize the extra effort involved in expanding the stiffened rib cage. This increased reliance on the diaphragm makes the ventilation of the old person especially sensitive to changes in intra-abdominal pressure, whether caused by a large meal or by body position.

The airways in a healthy old person offer no more resistance to airflow than those in a young person, so the work needed to overcome airway resistance is not increased. When a person is breathing quietly, the work required to shift air out of the lung during the expiratory phase is provided by the elastic recoil of the stretched lung. Since this recoil is less effective in the old person, expiratory flow velocities are reduced. Achievement of larger ventilated volumes involving invasion of the expiratory reserve volume calls for direct effort from the respiratory muscles. These muscles show the typical aging changes of skeletal muscle, a reduction in the size of motor units, and prolonged contraction and relaxation times, and they are therefore less able to provide adequate force to move air rapidly. As a consequence, all timed ventilatory functions, whether volumes moved per unit time (e.g., forced expira-

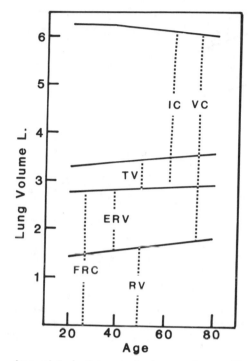

**Fig 5–2.**—Age-related changes in lung volume. The values are appropriate for a man 180 cm tall. (VC = vital capacity; IC = inspiratory capacity; TV = tidal volume; ERV = expiratory reserve volume; FRC = functional residual capacity; and RV = residual volume.)

tory volumes or maximal breathing capacity) or rates of airflow in some part of the expiration (e.g., mid-expiratory flow rate), decrease significantly in the aged individual who is free of lung disease (Fig 5–3).

The elasticity of the lung parenchyma maintains the patency of the small airways. At some point in an active expiration, pressures sufficient to close the small airways develop. The volume of air in the lung at this time is called the "closing volume." This closure phenomenon affects the basal parts of the lung to a greater extent than the more apical parts, since the latter are more stretched by the dependent weight of the lung. Consequently, the later parts of a forced expiration to residual volume are derived entirely from apical areas, which by virtue of their larger resting size receive

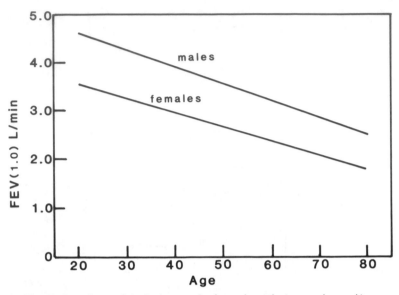

**Fig 5-3.**—Age-related change in forced expiratory volume (1 second) in men and women. $FEV_{(1.0)}$ is highly dependent on stature. The values given are for a man 180 cm tall and a woman 165 cm tall. (Based on data from Berglund E., Birath G., Burke J., et al.: *Acta Med. Scand.* 173:185–206, 1963.)

little of the preceding inspiration. The closing volume in a young person is greater than the residual volume but is still much less than the functional residual capacity. In the older person, the closing volume increases and may equal or even exceed the functional residual capacity. Consequently, some parts of the lung are unventilated for major parts of the breathing cycle.

The alveolar-arterial oxygen difference increases with age, but the alveolar $PO_2$ is virtually independent of age. This disequilibrium could arise from an increased shunt flow, a diffusion impairment, or a change in the ventilation/perfusion relationship. There is no evidence for an increase in the shunt flow over intrapulmonary channels via bronchial drainage or via thebesian veins. In regard to membrane effects, a linear decrease in the diffusing capacity for carbon monoxide with age is established, arising from a reduction in both the pulmonary capillary blood volume and the membrane area. However, a reduction in the diffusion capacity need not produce an elevated A-a$_{O_2}$ difference. That the phenomenon may be attributable in part to the uneven ventilation resulting from closure is supported by the observation that disequilibrium is less at large ventilated volumes when airways that would otherwise be closed are open and ventilation/perfusion uniformity is more nearly achieved.

In the lungs of older persons, the defense against inhaled particulate matter is reduced. Cilia are lost from the airways and the vigor of the remaining cilia is reduced. The "mucus escalator" thus becomes less effective in removing material from the peripheral lung. The macrophages that form the final line of defense at the alveolar level also become less efficient. The consequence for the old individual chronically exposed to particle-laden air is an additional decrease of oxygen uptake by occlusion of more of the already reduced alveolar surface. Although the hemoglobin concentration is maintained within normal limits in the healthy elderly person, there is a small alteration in red blood cell metabolism, which produces a decreased concentration of 2:3 diphosphoglycerate (DPG). As a consequence, the oxygen dissociation curve is shifted to the left, thus making the unloading of oxygen in the tissues more difficult (Fig 5-4).

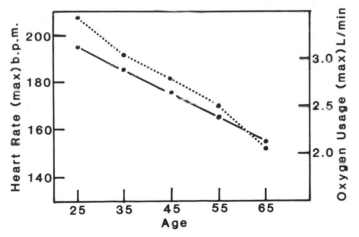

**Fig 5-4.**—The similar course of the decrease in maximum heart rate *(solid line)* and maximum oxygen consumption *(dotted line)* in aging men. b.p.m. = beats per minute. (Based on Astrand I., Astrand P.: in Folinsbee L.J., et al. [eds.]: *Environmental Stress,* New York, Academic Press, 1978, pp. 149-163.)

## Cardiovascular System

The heart and blood vessels are highly dependent for their normal function on the physical properties of distensibility, contractility, and elasticity, all of which involve connective tissue as well as muscle. Heart weight, expressed as a fraction of body weight, tends to increase slightly, although the capacity for stress-induced hypertrophy is reduced in older hearts. With aging, there is an increase in the ratio of collagen to muscle in the myocardium, which is located mostly in the immediate epi- and endocardial regions rather than generally throughout the chamber walls. However, the myocardium has a general increased stiffness rather than stiffness localized to these regions, and it has been suggested that the significant change is in the character of the connective tissue matrix rather than simply in the amount. The myocardial cells are a favored site for the deposition of the aging pigment lipofuscin, and the fraction of myocardial volume occupied by pigment increases linearly with age. Mitochondria increase in number and decrease in size.

The major structural alteration of the arteries is an increase in collagen and smooth muscle with some reduction in elastic tissue. As elsewhere in the body, the collagen tends to become cross-linked and calcium is deposited in the framework so generated. The intima thickens and is invaded by modified smooth muscle cells, which synthesize connective tissue proteins. The arteries show reduced compliance with age; the volume change produced by a pressure increase of 100 mm Hg at age 60 is only half of that in vessels of the 20-year-old. This loss of compliance represents a serious reduction in the capacity of the aorta to store part of the stroke volume, but it is compensated to some extent by an increase in aortic size. This expansion does not continue after age 60, however, with the consequence that the load on the left ventricle increases. The increase in arterial stiffness also leads to both an increase in the velocity of pulse wave transmission (which doubles between ages 20 and 60) and a decrease in the amplification of the arterial pulse between the aorta and the femoral artery. Veins become increasingly tortuous with age; the intima thickens and there is progressive fibrosis of the tunica media. The loss of elastic tissue weakens the vessel wall and varicosities occur in veins subjected to high pressure. Capillaries show a thickening of the basement membrane; fenestrations of the endothelium become fewer. These changes taken in association with the increasing density of ground substance of the connective tissue threaten adequate diffusional nutrition of the parenchyma.

The functional characteristics of the aging myocardium have been studied in isolated muscle preparations taken from experimental animals. Resting tension shows a greater rise with increasing length than it does in younger muscle, but there is no difference in the maximum isometric tension or the muscle length at which that tension is achieved. The time to peak isometric tension and the relaxation time increase with age. Muscle force and the velocity of shortening are reduced.

Some information about the contractile state of the human myocardium can be obtained noninvasively by measurement of the so-called systolic time intervals.

The time relationships of the systolic events of the cardiac cycle can be studied by the simultaneous recording of the ECG, the heart sounds, and the contour of the carotid pulse. The systolic time intervals so obtained are (1) the period of electromechanical systole (EMS) measured from the Q wave of the ECG to the start of the high-frequency component of the second heart sound and (2) the left ventricular ejection time (LVET) measured from the start of the rapid upstroke of the carotid pulse contour to the dicrotic notch. The difference between these intervals is the preejection period (PEP)—i.e., PEP = EMS − LVET.

Both EMS and LVET change inversely in a closely linear fashion with changes in the heart rate, so they are usually expressed as indices. For example, LVET index = LVET + $a$ × HR, where $a$ is the slope of the regression of LVET on heart rate and HR is heart rate. LVET or an index shows little change with age, but the PEP lengthens on the order of 15% between ages 25 and 65. As a consequence, EMS lengthens slightly over this age span. Lengthening of the PEP can result from a reduced inotropic state of the myocardium (a reduced resting sympathetic tonus), a reduced enddiastolic volume, or an alteration in the contractile properties themselves. It is likely that all three contribute, with the myocardial effect being the greatest. It is known that aged myofibrils have reduced activity of adenosine triphosphatase; in conjunction with changes in the intracardiac connective tissue, this may be basic to the extended contraction time of isolated cardiac muscle referred to earlier. The PEP also contains the time elements of excitation of the myocardium and excitation-contraction coupling. Although there is no evidence of reduced dromotropy (velocity of conduction of excitation) with age in the healthy heart, changes in the transverse tubule system of the cardiac muscle fibers could well modify the coupling time.

Cardiac output decreases approximately 1% per year in the age range of 20 to 80, while the stroke volume decreases 0.7% per year. These observations taken together imply a reduction in the resting heart rate, although direct investigations of the relationship of heart rate and age give no clear evidence of an increase or a decrease. The maximum heart rate that can be achieved, however, does change in a linear fashion with age and may be predicted from the relationship:

$$\text{Maximum HR} = 220 - \text{Age in years}$$

This reduction in chronotropic response may be the result of a change in the number of β-adrenergic receptors in the heart, a reduced release of neurotransmitters, or changes in the sinoatrial pacemaker cells as a result of the invasion of the node by fibrous tissue (Fig 5–5).

Bradycardia induced by breath holding in the end quiet expiratory position or by immersion of the face in water is significantly less marked in the old than in the young. This reaction is less in old individuals who are in good physical condition (particularly swimmers), and in fact the "aging" change can be seen in sedentary, unconditioned young people. This changed responsiveness is

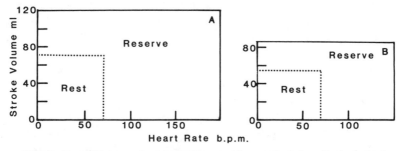

**Fig 5–5.**—Changes in the resting cardiac output (product of stroke volume and heart rate) and the reserve of function. **A,** 25-year-old man; **B,** 70-year-old man. b.p.m. = beats per minute.

interpreted as indicating a less effective vagal recruitment in the old or, again, a reduced responsiveness of the old sinoatrial node. Systolic time intervals recorded under these circumstances demonstrate that withdrawal of sympathetic stimulation occurs more slowly and to a lesser extent in the old. Following combined cholinergic and sympathetic blockade, the heart rate is slower in old than in young subjects. This indicates a reduced inherent sinus rhythm. The aged heart shows a reduced response of tachycardia to tilting, stemming probably from reduced baroreceptor sensitivity as a consequence of stiffening of the arterial wall.

Heart work tends to decrease slightly with age, while the total peripheral resistance increases steadily at a rate of little more than 1% per year. The tendency, therefore, is for perfusion to be decreased. The extent of decreased perfusion is variable among organs; in the kidney, it is dramatic (50%) as it is also in the splanchnic and cutaneous circulations. Cerebral blood flow (measured in milliliters of blood/minute/100 g of tissue) decreases by about 20% over 40 years. Changes in the resting flow to the myocardium and the skeletal muscle are less marked. However, the reaction of hyperemia following tissue hypoxia is significantly less in the old than in the young.

Many of the factors already discussed would be expected to increase arterial pressure, although the increase in aortic volume and the decrease in stroke volume would operate in the opposite direction. Longitudinal and cross-sectional studies have shown an increase in the systolic pressure with age, with a lesser rate of increase in the diastolic pressure. In the very old, diastolic pressure may fall. The rate at which the pressure rises correlates with blood pressure in the earlier years of life; the higher the initial pressure, the more rapid the rise. There are major questions, however, whether this increase in blood pressure is an inevitable consequence of healthy aging. Individuals who live in isolated, primitive societies do not show an increase in pressure as they age, nor do chronic psychiatric patients who grow old in a protected institutional environment. It may well be that the age-related rise in pressure is more a consequence of environmental factors, including diet and social stresses. Physical conditioning can slow or even reverse the rise; in some individuals, relaxation techniques reinforced by biofeedback are effective. Older persons fail to maintain the arterial pressure on tilting as might be expected in view of the diminished baroreceptor sensitivity, but there is no apparent effect of age on the rise of arterial pressure during exercise. Typical of the aging individual is a sluggishness in the return of both heart rate and blood pressure to resting levels following perturbation.

Figure 5–6 summarizes the effects of aging on the cardiovascular system.

## Physical Activity in Aging

In the previous sections, we have discussed the variety of changes that age produces in the ability of the body to acquire and

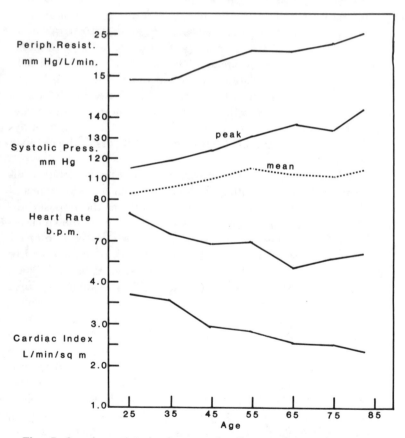

**Fig 5–6.**—Age-related changes in the cardiovascular system. (Based on data from Brandfonbrener M., Landowne M., Shock N.W.: *Circulation* 12:567–576, 1966.)

deliver oxygen to tissues. Each step in this pathway of oxygen is vulnerable, and the critical processes are as follows:

1. Ventilation: Reduced compliance of the respiratory apparatus leading to increased energy cost of breathing, reduced vital capacity and a substantially reduced maximum breathing capacity, and increased residual volume producing a poor alveolar ventilation coefficient.

2. Uptake of $O_2$: Ventilation-perfusion imbalance leading to less arterial saturation.

3. Transport of $O_2$: Reduced cardiac output and increased peripheral resistance leading to reduced perfusion, reduced ability of the microcirculation to dilate.

4. Utilization of $O_2$: Reduced active muscle mass, reduced arteriovenous difference for oxygen arising from a shift of the oxygen dissociation curve to the left as a consequence of reduced 2:3 DPG concentration, and reduced efficiency of the enzyme systems of active muscle.

Since these steps are arranged in series, it is not surprising that the physical work capacity of the average 70-year-old is only half that of a 20-year-old. Although the decrease is progressive over this age span, the rate of loss accelerates in the mid-50s. However, changes in physical capacity very similar to those occurring over a span of 25 years can be produced in a healthy young individual in only three weeks of enforced bed rest. Under these circumstances, the cardiac output decreases, the ventilatory capacity falls, adipose tissue is gained, lean muscle mass decreases, and mineral is lost from bone. Typically in the older person, especially after retirement from employment, physical activity is reduced, and it is apparent that in an analysis of the obvious reduction in physical capacity with age, three factors must be taken into consideration: (1) the presence of some early, undiagnosed pathology affecting the oxygen conductance system, (2) a genuine aging effect, and (3) the effect of what has been called "hypokinetic disease." Before the reality of hypokinetic disease was established, it was generally thought that little if any improvement of physical capacity could be expected from conditioning programs in older people. However, it has been shown that in fact older individuals are as trainable as younger ones in attaining a given percent change over the preconditioning status. Conditioning programs for older individuals must recognize the lessened flexibility in their cardiorespiratory systems. As an example, the range of heart rates available is narrowed by the reduction in the maximum heart rate with age. It has been shown, however, that conditioning can result from exercise that elevates the heart rate by as little as 40% of the available range (i.e., maximal heart rate to resting heart rate). This effectiveness threshold is lower than that in young people. For men in their 60s, this means there is a significant benefit from daily walking for 30 minutes at a speed sufficient to raise the heart rate to 100 or 110. More conditioning results from using more of the available heart rate range—e.g., 60%. It is prudent, however, to regard 75% of the available range as the "do not exceed" value for unsupervised activity. In addition to improving physical activity, conditioning has been shown to lower blood pressure in the hypertensive, reduce adiposity (increasing activity is often easier than reducing calorie intake), and have a tranquilizing effect that is useful in reducing tension.

## SUGGESTED READING

### RESPIRATORY SYSTEM

Campbell E.J., Lefrak S.S.: How aging affects the structure and function of the respiratory system. *Geriatrics* 33(6):68–78, 1978.

Holland J., Milic-Emili J., Macklem P.T.: Regional distribution of pulmonary ventilation and perfusion in elderly subjects. *J. Clin. Invest.* 47:81–82, 1968.

Lynne-Davies P.: Influence of age on the respiratory system. *Geriatrics* 32(8):57–62, 1977.

Mittman C., Edelman N.H., Norris A.H.: Relationship between chest wall and pulmonary compliance and age. *J. Appl. Physiol.* 20:1211, 1965.

### CARDIOVASCULAR SYSTEM

Brandfonbrener M., Lansdowne M., Shock N.W.: Changes in cardiac output with age. *Circulation* 12:557–566, 1955.

————: Relation of age to certain measures of performance of the heart and the circulation. *Circulation* 12:567–576, 1955.

Montoye H.J., Willis P.W., Howard G.E., et al.: Cardiac pre-ejection period: Age and sex comparisons. *J. Gerontol.* 26:208–216, 1971.

Norris A.H., Shock N.W., Yiengst M.J.: Age changes in heart rate and blood pressure responses to tilting and standardized exercises. *Circulation* 8:521–526, 1953.

## PHYSICAL ACTIVITY

Davies C.T.M.: The oxygen transporting system in relation to age. *Clin. Sci.* 42:1–13, 1973.

DeVries H.A.: Physiological effects of an exercise training regime upon men aged 52–88. *J. Gerontol.* 25:325–336, 1970.

Shephard R.J.: *Physical Activity and Aging.* Chicago, Year Book Medical Publishers, 1978.

# 6 / The Kidney and the Alimentary Tract

## Kidney

During development the kidney undergoes a series of regressions and remodelings that lead through the pronephros and mesonephros to the metanephros, which is established before birth. At birth, in spite of the small size of the organ, a full complement of nephron units has developed, and growth to adult size involves enlargements of the glomeruli and tubules, especially the proximal convoluted segment and the juxtamedullary units, which provide the long loops to the medulla. The adult kidney is capable of compensatory hypertrophy following, for example, the donation of a kidney, which appears to involve an enlargement of the nephron units without a change in their number. There is some evidence that in very young persons this may involve hyperplasia, whereas in older persons enlargement occurs by hypertrophy. The kidney reaches a maximum size in early adulthood and thereafter loses mass at a rate that increases markedly after age 50. Anatomical studies have shown that this age-related loss of mass involves the progressive deletion of entire nephron units, although a small number of aglomerular tubular systems (as many as 3%) have been reported in old kidneys (Fig 6–1).

The remodeling of the kidney that occurs during development appears to be induced by primary changes in the vasculature, and alterations in the pattern of perfusion have been suggested as the primary cause of the deletion of nephron units seen in aging. The major vascular alteration involves a reduction in the number of glomerular capillary loops, leading to the deletion of both the glomerulus and the associated peritubular plexus. An alternative pattern, seen mainly in juxtamedullary glomeruli, involves the formation of an arteriolar bypass of the degenerated glomerular capillaries (the Isaacs-Ludwig arteriole), which insures the continued perfusion of the vasa recta of the medulla. Arcuate and interlobar

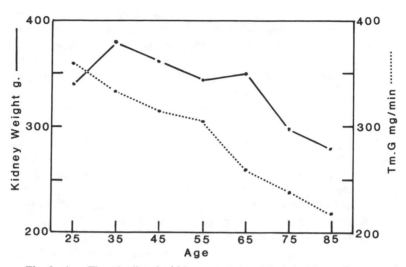

**Fig 6–1.**—The decline in kidney mass and in tubular maximum for glucose reabsorption. The similarity in the rates of decline supports the notion that age-related loss of renal substance comes about by loss of nephron units. $Tm_G$ values are standardized to a surface area of 1.73 sq m. (Based on data from Calloway N.O., Foley C.F., Lagerbloo P.J.: *Am. Geriatr. Soc.* 13:20–28, 1965; and Miller J.H., McDonald R.K., Shock N.W.: *J. Gerontol.* 7:196–200, 1952.)

arteries become tortuous, and although smaller arterial vessels show a loss of elastic tissue and a replacement of muscle by collagen, there is very little change in the lumen size. In the renal veins, the development of bundles of longitudinal muscle is a mark of aging; they are absent in children and present in 40% of the vessels of elderly individuals. Universally the basement membrane becomes thickened and there is an increase in the quantity of connective tissue. This is minor in the cortex but major in the medulla, where the large population of interstitial cells is replaced by extracellular material. From age 50 onward, there is a significant reduction in medullary hydration. These changes together with the loss of juxtamedullary glomeruli, which provide solute to the medullary osmotic stratification process, and the persistence of vasa recta perfusion account for the significant loss of concentrating ability in the old kidney.

Kidney weight remains stable from maturity until 40 years of age and then progressively decreases so that at age 80, the renal mass is only 70% of the adult value. Renal perfusion, however, is at its maximum in late adolescence, at which time the approximately 360 g of tissue receives 25% of the cardiac output (i.e., 1.25 L/minute). This peak perfusion decreases slowly over the next five years and thereafter remains stable until age 40, when a major linear decline begins. At age 80, perfusion is only 50% of that in the young adult. The glomerular filtration rate follows a similar course of decline but at a somewhat slower rate (Fig 6–2).

This change in the ratio of filtration rate to plasma flow (filtration fraction) may arise from a variety of causes. Since the estimate of the rate of plasma flow is made by measurement of the clearance of para-aminohippuric (PAH) acid or, in earlier studies, by Diodrast, a reduction in the secretory efficiency of the proximal tubules could give rise to a falsely low estimate of the plasma flow. Direct measurements of the arteriovenous difference for PAH, however, have shown no relationship with age. The increase in the filtration fraction, therefore, must be due to some anatomical or physiologic change in the glomerulus. It has been suggested that there is a preferential loss of cortical glomeruli, in which the filtration fraction is usually lower than in the juxtamedullary units. Another pos-

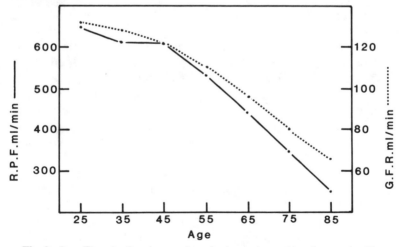

Fig 6–2.—The decline in renal perfusion rate and in glomerular filtration rate. Values are standardized to a surface area of 1.73 sq m. (Based on data from Davies D.F., Shock N.W.: *J. Clin. Invest.* 29:496–507, 1950.)

sible explanation is that there is a shift in the distribution of resistance offered by the glomerular arterioles either by an anatomical change in the lumen size or by a physiologic change in the tone of the arteriolar smooth muscle. One of the few effective means of increasing renal blood flow is by the administration of pyrogen. This technique applied to groups of young, middle-aged, and old subjects has demonstrated that in all three cases, the filtration fraction fell while the glomerular filtration rate remained stable. This indicates that the age-related decrease in the partial functions represents a matched loss of nephrons and vascular elements, and the age-related change in the filtration/perfusion ratio is due in part to a reversible alteration in the tone of the glomerular vessels.

Measurements of the maximal rate of secretory transport (Tm) for PAH or of reabsorptive transport for glucose are used to determine the available mass of the proximal tubular epithelium. Both these fall at a rate very close to the filtration rate, which is further confirmation of the loss of function by units. (See Fig 6–1.) However, the "splay" of these transport processes (the transition from total reabsorption or secretion to the plateau of saturated maximal transport) diminishes with age, suggesting that the nephron population has become more homogeneous.

As would be expected, the urea clearance falls at about the same rate as the filtration rate. Loss of concentrating ability has already been mentioned as a consequence of changes in the medullary structure and perfusion. It is also possible that in the aged, there is reduced responsiveness to vasopressin. The ability to form a dilute urine as measured by the clearance of osmotically uncommitted ("free") water is similarly depressed. As nephrons are progressively lost, the range of urine concentrations narrows and the condition of isosthenuria is approached (Fig 6–3).

A major problem of the aged kidney is its inability to handle either an acid or a base load. In part, this is the consequence of the reduced glomerular delivery of adequate amounts of bicarbonate and other buffers. The ability to form and excrete ammonia is reduced, but the amount of phosphate available for the formation of "titratable acidity" is slightly increased by a depression of the proximal reabsorption, possibly brought about by an elevation of the circulating level of parathyroid hormone, which is a consequence of a minor fall in the concentration of serum calcium. In

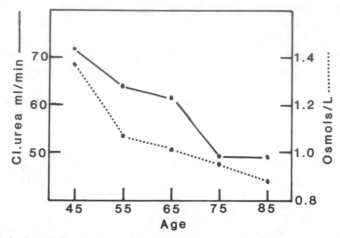

**Fig 6–3.**—Aging changes in maximal urea clearance and in limiting osmotic concentration of urine. Values for urea clearance are standardized to a surface area of 1.73 sq m. (Based on data from Lewis W.H., Alving A.S.: *Am. J. Physiol.* 123:500–515, 1938.)

spite of this, the aged kidney can maintain acid-base homeostasis at normal metabolic loads.

It should be borne in mind that renal functions are commonly reported standardized to a body surface area of 1.73 sq m. Depression of function with age seems to be less if reference is made to lean body mass. The fact that plasma creatinine levels rise by only 4% between ages 30 and 80 suggests that the basal function of the aged kidney is appropriate to the metabolism it serves.

### Alimentary Tract

One of the most important changes in the aging alimentary tract is the loss of teeth. In primitive man, this loss shortened lives, but today adequate dentures can maintain the masticatory function while diminishing somewhat the enjoyment of food. A survey in Sweden demonstrated a direct correlation between the hemoglobin level and the number of teeth, real or artificial. The link was provided by the direct correlation between meat consumption and the number of teeth.

The lining epithelial cells of the gut show the most rapid turnover rate of any body cells except for some of the leukocytes. One might expect that the diminished functional capacities of the aged would find expression in the gut. Animal studies have shown that the turnover rate of the epithelial cells diminishes with age, with the time from generation to shedding extended by about 25%.

## Motility

Although anatomical evidence of age-related changes in the gut is found largely in the mucosal layer, major alterations occur in motor function. In the esophagus, these changes are sufficiently regular and general to admit the term "presbyesophagus," involving both peristaltic and sphincteric elements.

The act of swallowing begins with relaxation of the upper esophageal sphincter and initiation of a traveling wave of peristalsis. (This is referred to as primary peristalsis in distinction from the secondary type, which clears the esophagus after gastroesophageal reflux.) Upon arrival of the peristaltic wave, the lower esophageal sphincter, which is maintained in a tonic state by humoral and chemical factors, relaxes until the wave has passed through it. In the old individual, peristaltic waves are not initiated by every swallow, and furthermore, the lower esophageal sphincter fails to relax with the arrival of each wave. In addition, the lower part of the esophagus shows ringlike contractions that are nonperistaltic (the so-called tertiary contractions). Manometric studies have shown that with age, total motor activity is not reduced but rather becomes uncoordinated. The net result of these changes is a delayed entry of food into the stomach, which is perceived as a sense of substernal fullness. This for many people substantially reduces the pleasure of a meal.

Gastric emptying time has not been directly studied but is known to be extended in persons who have atrophic gastritis, which affects both muscular and mucosal elements. The condition is certainly age related and may indeed be a normal aging change. Little is known about small-bowel motility in aging. Colonic dysfunction in the aged consists of constipation and diverticulosis. Constipation may be the result of diminished motor function, depression of the short reflexes of defecation, inadequate intake of fluid or bulk, neurologic disorder, or endocrine (thyroid) hypofunction. Diverticulosis, which consists of herniation of the colonic mucosa through the circular muscle layer and between the teniae coli, may result from an abnormal increase in the tone of the muscle coats, which generates abnormally high intraluminal pressure. So many and complex are the factors affecting the colonic function that it is impossible to isolate the pure effects of aging. Loss of tone affecting both internal and external anal sphincters is a major factor in fecal incontinence, which affects an increasing proportion of individuals in the later stages of aging.

### Secretion

After age 50, there is a reduction in salivary secretion and a reduction in the ptyalin content, which slows the early stages of digestion of complex carbohydrates.

The volume of gastric secretion in response to a test meal diminishes after age 40. This change is greater in men than in women. Resting acid secretion and secretion in response to a test meal or to histamine decrease after 50 years of age; again, the change is greater in men. When acid secretion rates are standardized on the basis of lean body mass or the exchangeable potassium pool, there is no decrease and, in fact, there may be an increase in women (Fig 6–4). Pepsin secretion diminishes between 40 and 60 years of age and then remains constant. The description of age-related changes in the stomach is complicated by the relatively high incidence of atrophic gastritis in older persons. This condition is

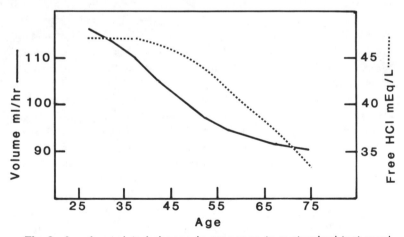

Fig 6–4.—Age-related change in response to a standard test meal. The declines shown occur only in men. In women, while there is a small decline in secretion rate, the concentration of free acid remains constant. (Based on data from Ivy A.C.: in Landry A.I. [ed.]: *Cowdry's Problems in Aging,* Baltimore, Williams & Wilkins Co., 1952.)

marked by an attenuation of both mucosa and muscle. In the extreme case, gastric glands may be totally lost and the mucosa takes on the appearance of the duodenum.

Neither the volume nor the bicarbonate content of pancreatic juice secreted in response to intravenous secretin is affected by age. Decreases have been reported in the concentration of pancreatic amylase and trypsin but not to a degree that would hinder carbohydrate or protein digestion. Pancreatic lipase is diminished in both resting and stimulated conditions but again appears to be adequate for normal levels of fat in the diet. There is no evidence that hepatic bile secretion is affected by age, but cholelithiasis is very common in the elderly. In this country, the incidence is estimated to be 10% in men and 20% in women older than 55.

## Absorption

There is no evidence that aging impairs absorption of the major nutrients, although such an impairment might be expected from the reduction in the mucosal area and perfusion that occur. Absorption is commonly tested by means of the sugar D-xylose, which uses the same pathway as the hexoses glucose and galactose. Absorption of D-xylose is independent of digestive enzymes and bile, so the test provides information about mucosal integrity and the adequacy of perfusion. The test, however, is based on the renal excretion of a dose given by mouth and so is really a test of both absorption and excretion. This test shows abnormal results in individuals older than 70, but it has been demonstrated that the defect is in the renal excretion of xylose (by glomerular filtration) rather than in absorption. No evidence has been found for impaired amino acid absorption, but a few studies have shown delayed lipid absorption. This appears to be due to reduced lipase activity rather than a mucosal defect.

After age 60, active absorptive transport of calcium declines and most people over age 80 show significant malabsorption. Iron and vitamins $B_1$ and $B_{12}$ appear to be less well absorbed in the old but not to the point of inadequacy.

### SUGGESTED READING

#### KIDNEY

Calloway N.O., Foley C.F., Langerbloom P.: Uncertainties in geriatric data. II. Organ size. *J. Am. Geriatr. Soc.* 13:20–28, 1965.

Davies D.F., Schock N.W.: Age changes in the glomerular filtration rate, effective renal plasma flow and tubular excretory capacity in adult males. *J. Clin. Invest.* 29:496–507, 1950.

Lewis W.H., Alving A.S.: Changes with age in the renal function in adult men. *Am. J. Physiol.* 123:500–515, 1938.

Lindeman R.D.: Age changes in renal function, in Goldman R., Rockstein M. (eds.): *Physiology and Pathology of Human Aging.* New York, Academic Press, 1975.

Papper S.: The effects of age in reducing renal function. *Geriatrics* 28(5):83–98, 1973.

Rowe J.W., Andres R., Tobin J.D., et al.: The effect of age on creatinine clearance in man: A cross section and longitudinal study. *J. Gerontol.* 31:155–163, 1976.

Wesson L.G.: *Physiology of the Human Kidney,* pp. 98–99. New York, Grune & Stratton, 1969.

ALIMENTARY TRACT

Calloway N.O., Merrill R.S.: The aging adult liver. *J. Am. Geriatr. Soc.* 13:594–598, 1965.

Fikry, M.E.: Exocrine pancreatic functions in the aged. *J. Am. Geriatr. Soc.* 16:463–467, 1968.

Geokas M.C., Haverback B.J.: The aging gastrointestinal tract. *Am. J. Surg.* 117:881–892, 1969.

Soergel K.H., Zboralske F.F., Amberg J.R.: Presbyesophagus: Esophageal motility in nonagenarians. *J. Clin. Invest.* 43:1472–1479, 1964.

# 7 / The Nervous System

## Anatomical Aging of the Brain

The weight of the brain reaches its peak of approximately 1.4 kg in the early 20s and then undergoes a slow decline. By age 80, the loss reaches 7%, or about 100 gm. This weight loss is accompanied by a reduction in the cortical area brought about by the broadening of sulci and a flattening of the gyri. This change is most apparent in the anterior halves of the hemispheres. There is no change in the size of the ventricles. Studies of hemispheric volume have shown a faster rate of loss in men than in women. During the aging process, the ratio of gray to white matter changes, indicating that there is some differential loss of cells and fibers. The ratio declines from ages 20 to 50 (predominant loss of cells) and then increases with further aging (predominant loss of fibers) (Fig 7–1). The hydration of brain tissue increases after age 70 but may decline again in the very old.

Cells are lost from the cerebral cortex at a rate that varies widely from area to area. The Golgi type II cells are particularly affected, and the pyramidal cells of layer 3 lose the horizontal association dendrites. In some areas, cell loss may be as great as 20% to 40%. The greatest loss occurs in the superior temporal gyrus, the precentral gyrus, and the area striata. The postcentral gyrus loses few or no cells. A similar loss occurs in the cerebellum but is later in onset than that in the cerebrum. The nuclei of the brain stem show no age-related loss of cells, with the exception of the locus ceruleus, where the loss begins only after age 65.

## Cellular Changes

Significant changes occur in both neurons and supporting cells. The major change affecting the axons is neuroaxonal degeneration, which is marked by the loss of myelin and swellings on the axis cylinders. This slow degenerative process, often referred to as "dying back," can be seen in 30% of old individuals, especially in

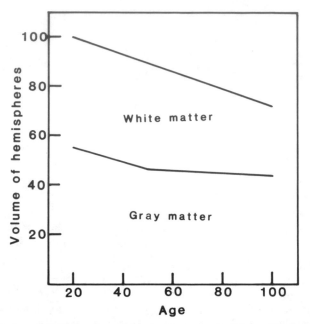

**Fig 7–1.**—Differing rates of loss of gray and white matter in the cerebral hemispheres. (Based on data from Terry R.D.: in Behnke J.A., Finch C.E., Moment G.B. [eds.]: *Biology of Aging,* New York, Plenum Press, 1978, p. 208.)

the posterior column system. Changes in the neuronal cell bodies take the form of inclusions and changes in microtubule structure. The most common inclusion is lipofuscin, which is distributed rather generally. Irregular membrane-bounded accumulations of protein fibrils occur commonly in the cells of the thalamus and brain stem. In the melanin-containing cells of the midbrain and brain stem, there are homogeneous hyaline bodies (Lewy bodies) 10 to 20 mμ with fine radiating strands. Cells of the hippocampus undergo granulovacuolar degeneration, in which clusters of vacuoles surround a dense central granule. These vacuoles may be the relics of lysosomes. After age 60, the number of neuronal microtubules may decrease and the depletion thereafter follows a linear course. This loss of normal microtubules is often accompanied by the appearance of so-called neurofibrillary tangles, which are in fact microtubules densely arranged in double helices. These tangles are a marked feature in cases of senile dementia of the Alzheimer type.

From age 60 onward, rounded foci of interstitial degeneration develop, the neuritic (senile) plaques. These may be scattered and solitary or they may coalesce. These plaques are found most commonly in the cortex and more rarely in the hypothalamus and limbic system; they have fine radiating strands, which are believed to be degenerated dendrites upon which amyloid is deposited.

Fibrillary astrocytes become more prominent with age, and the cells attach to blood vessels by enlarged foot processes. The substance amylopectin appears in the astrocytic processes in the form of the corpora amylacea. These bodies have a dense central core with a fibrillar border and are found most commonly in the immediate subpial cortex and near the linings of the ventricles. Within the choroid plexus, fibrils appear in both the epithelial cells and the ependymal cells. Especially prominent in the basal ganglia is an increase in the size of the perivascular space and a thickening of the walls of the small arteries.

In the peripheral nerves, there are fewer large fibers, and this is especially marked in the lumbosacral dorsal roots (Fig 7–2). In

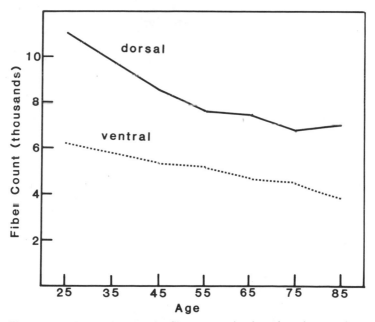

**Fig 7–2.**—Aging change in fiber count in dorsal and ventral roots (eighth thoracic segment). (Based on data from Corbin K.B., Gardner E.D.: *Anat. Rec.* 68:63, 1937.)

the efferent system likewise, the largest efferent fibers are lost. The consequences of this shift in the spectrum of fiber size are a slight change (5%) in the conduction velocity and the appearance of prolonged (polyphasic) muscle action potentials recorded with the electromyogram (Fig 7–3).

## Cerebral Blood Flow

In the young adult, the perfusion of the brain occurs at a rate of 50 to 60 ml/minute/100 gm of tissue; a little less than 40 ml/minute/100 gm is regarded as the necessary minimum to maintain full neuronal function. This marginal level of blood flow is approached in the very old, since the rate decreases 20% over the age span 30 to 70. The vertebral arteries tend to become tortuous with aging due to changes in the vertebrae and intervertebral disks and may become kinked with movements of the neck. This obstruction together with the already parlous perfusion may precipitate one variety of the transient ischemic attack to which many old persons are prone.

## Neurotransmitters

Typical of aging is the slowing of many neural processes. Most of this slowing occurs in central processes, where conduction over

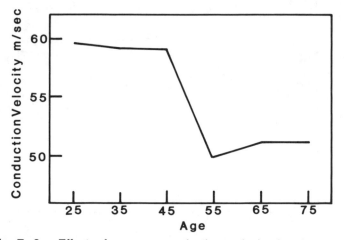

**Fig 7–3.**—Effect of age on conduction velocity in ulnar nerve. (Based on data from Wagman I.H., Leese H.J.: *Neurophysiology* 15:235, 1952.)

multisynaptic pathways is substantially delayed. The synaptic process depends on the liberation of a preformed chemical neurotransmitter substance from one neuron and the engagement of an appropriate receptor on the second neuron. Changes in the metabolism of neurotransmitter substances have profound effects on the activity of regulatory centers.

It is well established that parkinsonism is associated with a reduction in the amount of the monoamine dopamine in the basal ganglia. Dopamine is the neurotransmitter that provides communication between the cells of the substantia nigra and the corpus striatum. The occurrence of parkinsonism is strongly related to age, and the tremor and shuffling gate of the old may well be lesser manifestations of this same defect. Fortunately, "replacement therapy" is possible and is at least partially effective. L-Dopa, which can cross the blood-brain barrier, is converted in the brain into dopamine and norepinephrine. A limited number of studies in humans have shown that the level of enzymes concerned with catecholamine synthesis decreases with age, while the major enzyme involved in the disposal of the catecholamines, monoamine oxidase, increases in concentration in several parts of the brain. The concentration of norepinephrine in the hindbrain falls 40% to 50% between young adulthood and age 70. More extensive and detailed studies in experimental animals have confirmed this human evidence and further have shown that these changes in catecholamine synthesis occur in specific groups of cells. This implies that only some pathways are susceptible to change with aging. Catecholamines are involved as transmitters in the hypothalamic neurosecretion of releasing factors, especially the gonadotropin releasing factors. Since the liberation of releasing factors is modulated by the circulating levels of pituitary or other hormones, it has been speculated that catecholamine synthesis in certain hypothalamic sites is itself controlled by these hormones. A defect in this feedback system could then arise from an age-related change in the receptors of the synthesizing cells.

The demonstration of elevated levels of monoamine oxidase (MAO) in the aged has led to experimentation with MAO inhibitors (such as procaine hydrochloride) as an "elixir of youth." The results of such trials have been largely negative.

Acetylcholine, the major excitatory neurotransmitter in the cortex and limbic system, has also been studied in both experimental animals and humans. An impetus to these studies has been provided by the condition of senile dementia. This diagnosis, based on the signs of loss of initiative, loss of recent (short-term) memory, and difficulty with language and calculation, is made in about 10% of individuals older than 65. The impaired functions result from those areas of the brain in which acetylcholine is the transmitter substance. In many cases of senile dementia, a specific pathology can be demonstrated, but it is also likely that there is a true eugeric component. Most human studies have examined the concentration of choline acetyltransferase, the enzyme responsible for acetylcholine synthesis, rather than the neurotransmitter itself, which is too labile for postmortem study. Loss of acetylase activity is most marked in the cortex and in the caudate nucleus. The latter undergoes the major pathologic change in persons with Huntington's chorea, which has an incidence that is again strongly age related.

Glutamic acid decarboxylase, which is responsible for the formation of gamma-aminobutyric acid (GABA) from the precursor glutamic acid, undergoes a widespread, though modest, decline, which is most marked in the thalamus. This has led to speculation concerning the role of GABA cells in the processing of sensory information, which slows significantly in the old. There is a lack of information about the age-related alteration of other putative neurotransmitters.

### Aging of Reflexes

At the segmental level of spinal organization, the simple stretch reflexes are often depressed, and evidence from experimental animals has revealed a progressive increase in the central delay of these monosynaptic reflexes. Although this may be due to changes in the motor neuron itself, it could also arise from alterations in the input to the motor neurons from descending pathways. The plantar flexion and superficial abdominal reflexes also show an increase in central delay, often of considerable magnitude (e.g., 100 msec). Such changes in central delay, especially if cumulated over complex pathways, could account for a large part of the slowed motor response of old subjects, as tested, for example, by finger-tapping.

## Reaction Time

Reaction time is measured as the interval between the presentation of a visual or auditory signal and a motor response, such as pressing a button to terminate the signal. Reaction time thus encompasses the time involved in transduction of the signal, conduction to the central nervous system, processing, and initiation and conduction of a signal out to the appropriate responding muscle group (Fig 7–4). If an electromyogram (EMG) is recorded from the muscles involved, the time taken to make the motor response can be determined. Furthermore, the efferent conduction time can be estimated from a separate experiment to measure the conduction velocity of impulses in the motor nerve. Overall reaction time is longer by about 30% in old subjects (230 msec versus 170 msec). In part, this is due to a small reduction in the conduction velocity—approximately 2 msec. The "motor time" (time from the start of muscle activation as seen in the EMG to the completion of the movement) is prolonged in the older subject, probably due to less muscle power moving the finger slower. Joint stiffness also contributes to this effect. By far the greatest change, however, occurs in the central stages of processing. When motivation is provided by the threat of an electric shock delivered at a fixed interval after the stimulus, the age difference is slightly but not significantly reduced. Contributing to the lengthened central time in old subjects is probably an increase in synaptic delay time. In the rat, this increases 40% between young and old.

## Aging of the Senses

### Cutaneous Sense

Histologic studies have shown a progressive age-related decrease in the number of Meissner's corpuscles and a parallel de-

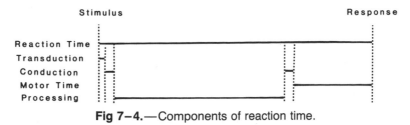

**Fig 7–4.**—Components of reaction time.

crease in the number of Pacinian and Kraus end organs as well as nerve fibers. As might be expected, sensitivity to light touch is decreased. The pain threshold does not change until late old age, when sensitivity appears to increase. This may be due to the skin becoming more deformable so that a stimulus can spread to involve more receptors. Temperature sensitivity in either direction from neutral is occasionally reduced (the evidence here is clinical rather than experimental). In contrast, there is a very clear increase in the vibratory threshold amounting to 50% for the fingers and tenfold for the great toe.

### Proprioceptive Sense

Older individuals require greater angular movements at the joints for perception to be achieved; this is especially true of the lower limb. Tests requiring duplication of a forced movement show impaired accuracy.

### The Special Senses

Aging changes occur early in the special senses. Vision, audition, and gustation all show a nearly linear impairment of function with age, beginning in early adulthood or before.

VISION.—The condition of presbyopia, the loss of range of accommodation for near vision, is perhaps the best known age-related change of the senses (Fig 7–5). The change is essentially a loss of flexibility of the lens, which fails to change shape appropriately when the tension of the suspensory ligaments decreases with contraction of the ciliary muscle. The lens continues to grow but more slowly throughout life, and between ages 20 and 80, the anterior-posterior diameter of the lens increases by 50%. Growth consists of the laying down of new cells on the surface of the lens. At the same time, the central cells lose their cellular identity and become crystalline. In this now acellular part of the lens, microopacities develop. Although these do not affect visual acuity, they produce a "dusty windshield" effect and small bright light sources produce dazzle. This continuing growth of the lens results in not only a loss of lens flexibility but also a reduction in the size of the anterior chamber and some consequent impairment of the circulation of aqueous humor leading to increased intraocular pressure. The aging individual becomes aware of the loss of accommodation by a very obvious change in the distance from the eye at which type can be read. This "nearpoint," which is about 10 cm at age

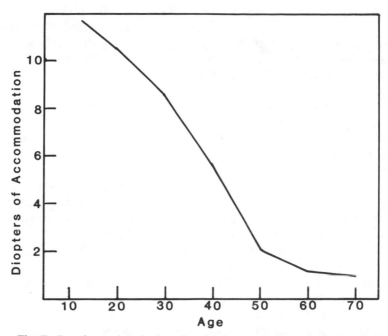

**Fig 7–5.**—Age-related alteration in the available range of accommodation. (Based on data from Friedenwald J.S.: in Lansing A.I. [ed.]: *Cowdry's Problems in Aging,* Baltimore, Williams & Wilkins Co., 1952.)

20, recedes to 100 cm by age 70. In addition, the speed with which accommodation is performed declines, due probably to the loss of contractile force in the ciliary muscle or a change in the motor control of the muscle.

The vitreous body loses hydration, and the concentric sheets that provide the skeleton for the mucoid component tend to separate. This may lead to a loss of the important tampon function of the vitreous on the retina and the appearance of "floaters" in the visual field.

The pupil becomes smaller with aging, and the range of dilation and constriction in response to changed levels of illumination is much less. At age 60, the amount of light incident upon the retina is only one third of that at age 20, with a consequent rise in the visual threshold for light perception as well as in the level of illumination necessary for reading.

Receptors are lost, which chiefly affects the rods of the peripheral retina. This, together with a sinking of the eye into the orbit and some degree of ptosis, significantly reduces the size of the visual field. There is a minor loss of receptors of the fovea sufficient to produce a loss of visual acuity even when the aging changes in refraction have been completely corrected.

The chemical processes of vision become impaired so that dark adaptation occurs more slowly and to a lesser total extent. The aqueous humor becomes pigmented and acts as a yellow filter, leading the old person to have difficulty matching blues and greens.

In the old person, there is a decrease in the "critical fusion frequency"—that is, the least frequency of flashing of a light that is perceived as an uninterrupted signal. This effect indicates a longer persistence of the "trace" of the stimulus in the old.

HEARING.—Almost all the components of the auditory system change with aging. There is a loss of elasticity in the tympanic membrane, impaired articulation of the ossicles, loss of elasticity in both the basilar and Reisner's membrane, loss of hair cells and supporting cells from the organ of Corti, and loss of neurons from the temporal cortex. Degenerative changes in the stria vascularis of the cochlea are also common.

Hearing is at its most efficient, in both acuity and range of perceivable frequencies, at age 10. At 10, one can hear sounds with frequencies as high as 20 kHz; by age 50, this upper limit is only 14 kHz, and by age 60, there is little useful hearing above 5 kHz (Fig 7–6). This decline in sensitivity for the higher frequencies is observed in testing by both air and bone conduction. This locates the impairment central to the outer or middle ear. Shrinkage of the frequency range is accompanied by loss of acuity (amounting to 40 to 50 dB) for all frequencies higher than 1,000 Hz (Fig 7–7). Although pure-tone hearing in the speech frequency range is only moderately attenuated, there is a loss of speech reception much greater than might be predicted, which is attributable perhaps to changes in the central processing of the signals. Auditory reaction times are increased and there is some loss of sound orientation, again suggesting poor central processing.

In some individuals, with the loss of pure-tone perception, "noise" develops in the auditory circuitry, producing the persistent ringing sensation of tinnitus. More rarely, the elevation of the

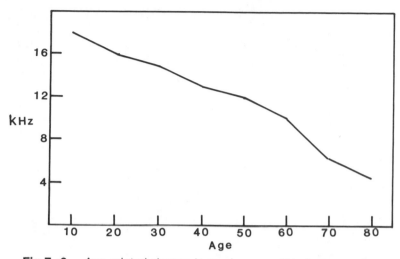

**Fig 7–6.**—Age-related change in maximum audible frequency (measured at submaximal intensity). (Based on data from Schober F.W.: *Akut. Beih.* 4:219, 1952.)

threshold for hearing is accompanied by an enhanced "recruitment" of perceived intensity after the threshold has been reached. In extreme cases, this may result in pain as a consequence of amplifying sound into the audible range.

TASTE.—With age, the taste papillae degenerate and the number of taste buds within each papilla is reduced. Some reports have placed the loss as high as 70% between childhood and age 80. Studies using the conventional battery of test substances—sugar, salt, hydrochloric acid, and quinine—have produced results that are divided almost equally between a significant increase in the taste threshold and no change. However, tests in which a controlled galvanic current was used to stimulate receptors (the current produces a metallic or acid taste) have demonstrated a rather linear increase in the threshold starting in young adulthood and reaching a fivefold decrease in sensitivity by age 80. The loss of taste sensation is also exacerbated by the reduced flow and reduced amylase content of the saliva.

SMELL.—There is anatomical evidence of an age-related loss of neurons in the olfactory bulb, but few systematic tests of olfactory sensitivity have been made. One such study showed a marked age-

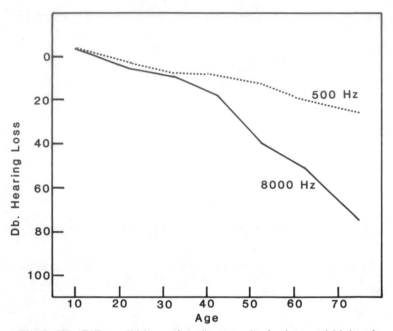

**Fig 7-7.**—Differential loss of auditory acuity for low and higher frequencies. (Based on data from Rosee B.: *Z. Laryngol. Rhinol. Otol.* 32:414, 1953.)

related elevation of the detection threshold for four common odors—coffee, oil of peppermint, oil of almonds, and coal tar.

The suggestion has been made that the losses in audition, olfaction, and gustation have a common component in neuronal degeneration in the lower part of the postcentral gyrus where the sensations are appreciated.

## Vestibular Function

The vestibular apparatus of old individuals shows a significant loss of hair cells of the cristae ampullaris as well as a loss of supporting cells. Degeneration of the macula has also been described in both the saccule and the utricle. However, tests of vestibular function both by the caloric test and by rotation have given confusing results. In both tests, assessment of vestibular function is based on parameters of the induced nystagmus—duration, amplitude, and frequency. There have been reports of age-related reductions in sensitivity, age-related increases, and a total lack of relation to age. However, when assessment is based on the maximum values for velocity, amplitude, or frequency of the induced nystagmus, the greatest sensitivity is found in middle-aged persons, with lesser sensitivity in young adults and older persons. These tests do not necessarily address the effects of age on the vestibular input to balance and posture, since central integration and processing are not involved to the same extent in the production of nystagmus. Old persons certainly appear to be more resistant than the young adult to motion sickness.

## Balance and Posture

The precision with which the motor system can maintain a stable posture is commonly judged by the extent of "sway" of the body when the person is standing with eyes closed. Old people show exaggerated sway. The more demanding test of maintaining balance while standing on one leg is impossible for many of the elderly. Contributing to this impairment of balance are the loss of proprioceptive input, both conscious and unconscious, the loss of cells from the cerebellum, and probably some loss of vestibular input because of the degenerative changes of the saccule and the utricle.

## Gait

The gait of an old person tends to be slow, often on a widened base, and shuffling rather than brisk. Loss of muscle mass and strength of the legs, changes in the pattern of activation of muscle that follow the loss of large motor nerve fibers, and the stiffening of joints all combine with proprioceptive impairment to produce this picture.

## Tremor

Tremor may arise from many changes within the nervous system. The resting tremor of parkinsonism has been identified as resulting from an inadequacy of the transmitter substance, dopamine, in the nigrostriatal system. The incidence of this condition is strongly related to age. Tremor may also arise from damage to the comparator function of the cerebellum. This "intention tremor," which is part of the general phenomenon of dysmetria, follows the loss of adequate proprioceptive input as well as the loss of cerebellar neurons. All individuals when asked to maintain a limb in a steady position, for example, show some degree of tremor. This is often referred to as "physiologic tremor." In children, the dominant frequency of the tremor is close to 6 Hz. This increases to approximately 10 Hz in the adult and then with further aging falls again to the childhood value. One explanation proposed for this decreased frequency is a central synchronization of motor activity. In old people, clonus can be more readily elicited than in the young. This response to the maintained stretch of a muscle has been attributed to decreased serotonin activity within the olivodentate system.

The general picture of the aging nervous system is declining efficiency involving both the transducer system of receptors (e.g., the thickening lens and sclerosing ossicles of the ear) and the nervous system elements themselves. A reduction in the number of both central and peripheral neurons limits the flow of information in the system, and the remaining elements must transmit signals for a longer time to allow for summation to the threshold level. This repeated at each stage of a complex information channel accounts for the increased central processing time that occurs. Furthermore, a reduced number of neurons within the system decreases the functional reserve, thus leading potentially to information overload and confusion of signals. In addition, the aged nervous system requires longer to "clear the decks" to take up a new response (reflected, for example, in the change in the critical fusion frequency). An old person is at a disadvantage when speed is called for in a receptive task. This topic arises again in relation to the higher cortical functions (see chap. 10).

## SUGGESTED READING

Engen T.: Taste and smell, in Birren J.E., Schaie K.W.(eds.): *Handbook of the Psychology of Aging*. New York, Van Nostrand Reinhold, 1977, pp. 554–559.

Finch C.E.: Neuroendocrine and autonomic aspects of aging, in Finch C.E., Hayflick L. (eds.): *Handbook of the Biology of Aging*. New York, Van Nostrand Reinhold, 1977, pp. 262–274.

Hanley T.: Neuronal fallout in aging brain: A critical review of the quantitative data. *Age Ageing* 3:133–151, 1974.

Mulleh G., Peterman W.: Influence of age on results of vestibular function tests. *Ann. Otol. Rhinol. Laryngol.* 88 (suppl. 56), 1979.

Terry R.D., Gershon S. (eds.): *Neurobiology of Aging*. New York, Raven Press, 1976.

————.Brody H.: An examination of cerebral cortex and brain stem aging, pp. 177–182.

————.McGeer E., McGeer P.L.: Neurotransmitter metabolism in the aging brain, pp. 389–404.

————.Straehler B.L.: Introduction: Aging and the human brain, pp. 1–22.

————. Cerebral blood flow, EEG and behavior in aging, pp. 103–120.

Timiras P.S., Vernadakis A.: Structural, biochemical and functional aging of the nervous system, in Timiras P.S. (ed.): *Developmental Physiology and Aging*. New York, Macmillan Publishing Co., 1972, pp. 502–526.

Weiss A.D.: Sensory functions, in Birren J.E. (ed.): *Handbook of Aging and the Individual*. Chicago, University of Chicago Press, 1959, pp. 503–542.

# 8 / The Endocrine System and the Reproductive System

## The Endocrine System

The endocrine system is central to so many of the body's regulatory and adaptive mechanisms that it is tempting to assign a major role in the loss of homeostatic competence in the aged to alterations in the endocrine glands. Apart from the hormonal changes that accompany the female menopause, however, functional alterations in aging endocrine glands tend to be subtle and frequently can be revealed only by challenges to the regulatory and feedback systems of the hypothalamus and pituitary.

### Pituitary

In man, the pituitary does not lose a significant amount of weight with aging, but there is a reduction of vascularity and an increase in the content of connective tissue. The eosinophil cells (concerned with growth hormone and prolactin production) decrease in number, while the chromophobe cells proliferate.

GROWTH HORMONE.—The amount of growth hormone in the anterior pituitary does not change with age. Studies on the effect of aging on circulatory levels of the hormone are complicated by sex differences and by the blunted secretion in obese subjects. Old persons do not show the bursts of secretion during sleep that are seen in young individuals, and this has been correlated with the loss of the slow-wave sleep pattern in the old. In old subjects, exercise fails to provoke secretion and provocative tests using either insulin hypoglycemia or arginine injection likewise show a reduced response. It is highly probable that these reduced secretory responses relate more to adiposity than to age.

PROLACTIN.—Serum levels of prolactin in men do not change with age, but in women, a decline begins at the menopause. The pituitary content of prolactin in postmenopausal women is higher than in men. Prolactin secretion in response to provocation is delayed in onset but persists longer in the older subject.

THYROTROPIN.—There appears to be no age-related change in the plasma level of thyrotropin. When the secretory response to synthetic releasing hormone is tested, the response to a given dose is significantly lower in old subjects. This may reflect either a reduced sensitivity of the system to the releasing factor or an absolute reduction in secretory capacity.

CORTICOTROPIN.—No change occurs in the pituitary content of ACTH with age; the circadian rhythm of circulating levels shows no change and the release in response to stress remains intact. Tests of feedback suppression of secretion by circulating steroids (the dexamethasone test) also show no age-related change.

VASOPRESSIN.—Circulating levels of the antidiuretic hormone in response to osmotic challenge tend to be higher in old persons than in the young. This is probably due to a reduction in the renal and hepatic clearance of the hormone rather than to a change in secretion.

## Adrenal Cortex

There is a slight loss of adrenal weight that begins at about age 50 and is accompanied by an increase in connective tissue, which replaces parenchymal cells and produces a thickening of the capsule. Pigment accumulates throughout the cortex and the amount of lipid in the zona fasciculata is reduced. There is also a tendency for the demarcation of the three cortical zones to become more diffuse.

Plasma glucocorticoid levels are similar in young and old individuals; both show the same pattern of diurnal variation, with the highest values observed in the early morning and low values in the evening. Glucocorticoid concentration measured in the middle of the night, however, tends to be significantly higher in the old than in the young. The distribution of the glucocorticoids does not change with age, but there is a significant depression of the disposal rate. Since the plasma concentration is not dependent on age, the lower rate of disposal matches a lower rate of secretion. The response of the adrenal cortex to ACTH remains normal in old people, and the pituitary release of ACTH in response to stress is likewise intact.

Circulating levels of aldosterone are lower in the old than in the young. Aldosterone secretion is controlled by the renin-angiotensin system, by the plasma potassium concentration, and to only a small extent in man by ACTH. In the old, there is a depressed response of the renin-initiated system both to acute alterations in blood volume distribution (e.g., posture) and to chronic salt and water depletion. The response to ACTH is not affected by age. Secretion of the adrenal androgens decreases with age, but since no clear functional role has been assigned to these hormones, the significance is unknown.

## Pancreas

The weight of the pancreas remains stable throughout adulthood and into old age. Very little is known about age-related alterations in the fine structure because of the extremely rapid autolysis the tissue undergoes.

## Insulin

Resting levels of insulin secretion remain stable with age, but deterioration of glucose tolerance as demonstrated by the usual tests begins in middle adulthood and progresses steadily with age. The blood glucose level two hours after a 50-g oral dose of glucose increases about 6% for each decade; thus, half of older subjects display a tolerance curve outside the norm plus two standard deviations in young adults. Since the prevalence of adult-onset diabetes increases with age, it is difficult to differentiate between physiologic decline and a genetic trait. The questions that arise from the observation of the low glucose tolerance are: (1) Is there a reduced response of the β-cell to the glucose load? and (2) Is there a change in tissue sensitivity to insulin? The application of the glucose clamp technique, in which the plasma glucose concentration is servocontrolled, has led to the conclusion that β-cell sensitivity is indeed decreased in older individuals. The intravenous insulin tolerance test of peripheral sensitivity to insulin shows this to be unchanged with age. The possibility also exists that in older people, a larger fraction of the immunoreactive insulin is in fact the biologically inactive precursor proinsulin.

## Glucagon

Information on age-related changes in glucagon secretion is very limited. The fasting plasma level does not change with age nor is there a reduction in the increase following arginine provocation. One study has shown that the rise in the blood glucose level in response to the administration of exogenous glucagon is both delayed in time and reduced in magnitude.

## Thyroid

Although significant changes occur in thyroid structure with age—for example, reduced follicular diameter, reduced epithelial cell height, and reduced amount of colloid—its function appears to remain adequate. Although the basal metabolic rate declines steadily with aging, this change does not occur when caloric output is standardized to total body water or lean body mass rather than to surface area. There is a slight reduction in the concentration of TBG (thyroxin binding globulin), but the serum concentration of thyroxine ($T_4$) remains essentially unchanged. The concentration of triiodothyronine ($T_3$) diminishes significantly with age, and this has been attributed to a reduced conversion of $T_4$ to $T_3$ in extrathyroidal locations. The disposal rate of $T_4$ is reduced as a consequence of the declining activity of hepatic enzyme systems or a lack of strenuous physical activity, which is a powerful stimulant to disposal. In old men, but not in old women, secretion of the pituitary trophic factor TSH is reduced in response to the hypothalamic releasing factor TRH. In both sexes, direct stimulation of thyroid secretion by TSH or by fever shows the responsiveness of the gland to be unchanged with age. The retention of a normal circulating level of $T_4$ with a reduced rate of disposal suggests that the feedback control system has been readjusted.

## Parathyroid

The major aging structural change in the parathyroid is an increase in the interstitial adipose tissue. The accumulation of fat may account for as much as 40% of the weight of the gland. There is a striking difference between the sexes in the pattern of change in the circulating levels of parathormone with age. In men, the level starts out low and increases until the sixth decade; the circulating level in individuals in their 50s is about three times that seen in the 20s. After the peak in the 50s levels decline back toward the values found in young men. Young women, on the other hand, have a circulating level about twice that in young men. The value declines to its lowest in the 40s and then climbs steadily with further aging with no sign of the decrease seen in men. This progressive rise after middle age in women is exaggerated in those who develop postmenopausal osteoporosis. The major route of disposal of the hormone is degradation in the kidney, and in experimental animals, it has been shown that this process slows with age.

The changed circulating levels thus reflect the interaction of changes in the rates of both secretion and elimination.

## The Reproductive System

The human female is unique in that the cessation of reproductive capability is not associated with death. Today a woman can expect to live for about 28 years after the menstrual cycle ceases. The cessation of the reproductive function is a dramatic manifestation of aging in a major physiologic system. Associated with the loss of cyclic changes in the levels of the sex hormones, numerous imbalances occur in neural and endocrine regulatory mechanisms, which together form the female climacteric. In men, no episode in aging corresponds to the female menopause. Reproductive function shows a slow progressive decline rather than an abrupt termination. As a consequence, men normally have no climacteric, although some metabolic and neuroendocrine imbalances are found in hypogonadic men.

### Ovary

From the prenatal period onward, oocytes are lost from the ovary, and by the time of menarche only 10% of the primordial follicles that were in the fetal ovary remain (Fig 8–1). From the age of 30 onward, ovarian weight decreases, the quantity of connective tissue increases, and perfusion diminishes. With aging, there is also a reduction in the number of follicles that undergo normal growth and development. Many show maturational defects possibly indicative of a lowered responsiveness of the ovary to the gonadotropins. Before the onset of the menopause, there is a reduced formation of corpora lutea. Since these are essential to the maintenance of pregnancy, women have lower fertility and higher rates of miscarriage in these years. Ova formed in the later reproductive life have diminished viability and higher rates of chromosomal abnormality. As menopause is approached, cycles become irregular and ova may become "overripe," another cause of chromosomal abnormality.

### Female Secondary Sex Organs

Adequate circulating levels of the sex hormones are essential to the maintenance of the secondary organs. The uterus reaches its peak weight at age 30 and by age 50 has lost half its mass. There

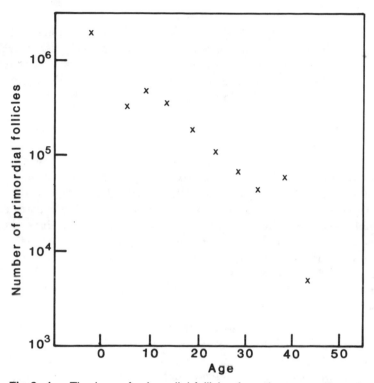

**Fig 8–1.**—The loss of primordial follicles from the ovary. (Based on data from Beck E.: *Acta Anat.* 14:108, 1952.)

is a major loss of both collagen and elastin, and the remaining collagen shows the typical aging changes attributed to the development of cross-linking. The fallopian tubes also shrink. The vagina shrinks and the wall thins. In the presence of decreased estrogen activity, the vaginal lining is reduced to a single layer of flattened cells and there may be patches of erosion. Drying and keratinization occur in the vaginal outlet, and the labia and clitoris diminish in size. Loss of pubic hair occurs late in the aging process. In the mammary glands, alveoli are lost and the size of the ducts decreases as their lining thins. There is often some loss of adipose tissue. This loss of mass together with the aging changes in the connective tissue leads to flaccid and drooping breasts. The nipples shrink and lose their ability to become erect.

## Testis

There is little or no loss of weight of the testis with aging, but there is an increase in the fibrous tissue of the intertubular spaces. The basement membrane around the seminiferous tubules thickens. Of the three cell types of the testis, germinal cells, Sertoli's cells, and the interstitial cells of Leydig, the latter show the greatest change with age. These cells, which are the source of testosterone and androgens, accumulate lipid from puberty to approximately age 30. From this time onward, cells are lost and the remaining cells show a decreased lipid content that correlates well with the decline observed in androgen excretion. By contrast, Sertoli's cells continue to accumulate lipid throughout life, and this is suggested to be related to estrogen production. Sperm production continues into advanced old age, but the rate slows and there is an increase in the proportion of abnormal forms. Active spermatozoa are present in the ejaculates of 70% of men 60 to 70 years of age and in 50% of the ejaculates of men 80 to 90 years old, although in this older group, the sperm count is only 50% of that in the young adult.

## Male Secondary Sex Organs

Changes begin to appear in the prostate of men from age 40 onward. First, there are diffuse changes in part of the gland; then smooth muscle atrophies and is replaced by denser connective tissue; the columnar epithelium is converted to cuboidal forms and concretions (corpora amylacea) appear in the ducts. As aging progresses, these changes encompass the whole gland. Acini are lost and connective tissue continues to accumulate, leading to the common prostatic hypertrophy. The seminal vesicles accumulate granular pigment, some of which finds its way into the semen.

## Reproductive Hormones

Although the phenomena of reproductive aging in men and in women are so different, the changes in the sex hormones are generally similar. Both the ovary and the testis show a reduced responsiveness to the pituitary gonadotropins, and the stage is thus set for a positive feedback system. The urinary excretion of estrogens in women and of androgens in men decreases rapidly beginning in the young adult years. In men, this fall is interrupted in middle age but then the level drops precipitously after age 65. In women, estrogen excretion falls steadily until the sixth or seventh decade and then tends to plateau. The estrogens present at this time do not originate in the ovary. The decrease in the amounts of estrogens and androgens leads by way of reduced negative feedback at the pituitary to an increased production of the gonadotropins. This increase is three times greater in women than in men. Although there is a substantial decrease in androgen production by Leydig's cells in the testis, the continued estrogenic activity of Sertoli's cells maintains some negative feedback on the production of

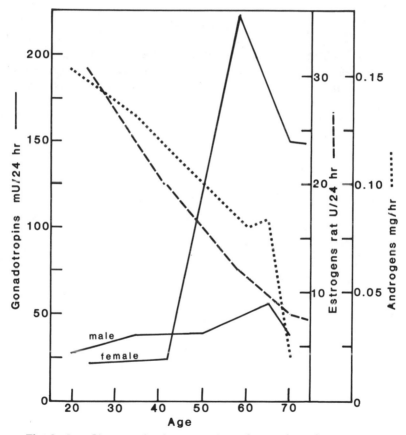

**Fig 8-2.**—Changes in the excretion of gonadotropins, estrogens, and androgens with age. mU = milliunits. (Based on data from Pincus G., et al.: *J. Gerontol.* 9:113, 1954; and Johnsen S.G.: *Acta Endocrinol.* 31:209, 1959.)

gonadotropins. The plateau of androgen production in middle age tends to delay the rise in the level of gonadotropins relative to that in women (Fig 8–2).

## The Climacteric

Although the climacteric is not a universal phenomenon, most women experience a complex of symptoms in the years immediately following the menopause. These symptoms of the "change of life" include vasomotor instability marked by "hot flushes" most commonly in the dermatomes of the cervical segments, outbursts of sweating, paroxysmal tachycardia, and chills. Emotional changes, bouts of depression, and withdrawal from family also occur but less frequently. The postmenopausal period is also marked by an imbalance in osteoclastic and osteoblastic activity, which leads to a large incidence of osteoporosis. Although not confined to women, the extent of this loss of bone mineral is much less in men. The menopause also leads to changes in the secretion pattern of growth hormone; the morning peak is lost. Since the climacteric is a unique human phenomenon, no animal model exists for investigation of the syndrome. However, evidence from rats has led to a proposal that the link between estrogen deficiency and the postmenopausal syndrome might be provided by some neurotransmitters that can be modulated in activity by the ovarian steroids. Such modulation has been demonstrated for the catecholamines and the prostaglandins. The postmenopausal symptoms last for only months or, in the extreme case, for a few years. Presumably this termination of the syndrome is brought about by other non-estrogen-modulated changes in neurotransmitter synthesis and disposal that occur as aging progresses (see chap. 7).

## SUGGESTED READING

### ENDOCRINE SYSTEM

Audres R., Tobin J.D.: Endocrine systems, in Finch C.E., Hayflick L. (eds.): *Handbook of the Biology of Aging.* New York, Van Nostrand Reinhold, 1977, pp. 357–358.
Greenblatt R.B.: *Geriatric Endocrinology.* New York, Raven Press, 1978.
————.Blichert-Toft M.: The adrenal glands in old age, pp. 81–102.
————.Ingbar S.H.: Influence of aging on the human thyroid hormone economy, pp. 13–32.
————.Mills T.M., Mahash V.B.: Pituitary function in the aged, pp. 1–12.

Roof B.S., Piel C.F., Hansen J., et al.: Serum parathyroid hormone levels and serum calcium levels from birth to senescence. *Mech. Ageing Dev.* 5:289–304, 1976.

REPRODUCTIVE SYSTEM

Andrew W.: *The Anatomy of Aging in Man and Animals.* New York, Grune & Stratton, 1971, pp. 183–193.

Finch C.E.: Endocrine and neural factors of reproductive aging—a speculation, in Terry R.D., Gershon S. (eds.): *Neurobiology of Aging.* New York, Raven Press, 1976, pp. 335–338.

Greenblatt R.B.: *Geriatric Endocrinology.* New York, Raven Press, 1978.

———.Asch R. H., Greenblatt R.B.: The aging ovary: Morphologic and endocrine correlations, pp. 141–164.

———.Rakoff A.E., Nowroozi K.: The female climacteric, pp. 165–190.

Timiras P.S., Meisami E.: Changes in gonadal function, in Timiras P.S. (ed.): *Developmental Physiology and Aging.* New York, Macmillan Publishing Co., 1972, pp. 527–541.

Yen S.S.C.: The biology of the menopause. *J. Reprod. Med.* 18:287–296, 1977.

# 9 / Aging of Regulatory Mechanisms

AMONG THE THEORIES of aging that were previously mentioned was that of impairment of the body's homeostatic regulatory system. Our examination of the organ systems has shown limitations of function that are often due to changes in the effector tissues. In other instances, function appears to be impaired by inadequate input of information from receptor systems. The central elements of regulation are also susceptible to age-related changes. Among these elements are the autonomic nervous system and its higher centers together with the endocrine system and the neurotransmitter substances. The latter have already been considered.

## Autonomic Nervous System

In spite of its name, this division of the nervous system is not autonomous but rather operates largely as the efferent limb for the reflexes that are responsible for the maintenance of certain aspects of homeostasis. Autonomic regulation of function, therefore, is vulnerable to the aging process at each link in the reflex arc—at the receptor, in the integrating neural centers, in the ganglia, and at the effector terminations.

Information on the changes that occur in this system in man is at best fragmentary, but animal experiments have provided some indication of these changes. This work has shown that with age, greater intensities of stimulation must be applied to sympathetic or parasympathetic nerves to elicit a change in the end organ. At the autonomic ganglia, sensitivity to preganglionic stimulation is lost and there is a reduction in the maximum frequency with which impulses can be transmitted through the ganglionic synapses. At the same time, end organs and ganglia show an increased sensitivity to neurotransmitters applied directly. This phenomenon is clearly related to "denervation hypersensitivity." With aging, there is a reduction in the number of nervous system elements and reduced neurotransmitter synthesis. In the cholinergic parts of the system, the ganglia and the muscarinic terminations, the reduced rate of synthesis is accompanied by a decreased concentration of acetylcholinesterase. The effect of this is to protect the function of the end organ. The balance between reduced synthesis and reduced disposal differs from organ to organ so that hypersensitivity is a variable phenomenon. Old ganglia also have an increased sensitivity to blocking agents such as hexamethonium. In the adrenergic system, on the other hand, the postsynaptic elements show a reduced sensitivity to excitatory and blocking agents. For example, the adrenergic agonist isoproterenol produces less vasodilation in vessels of the old than in those of the young. This is apparently not due to a change in the vessel wall, since dilation in response to nitrite is not impaired. One possibility is that the receptor density changes with age. The smooth muscle of the aortic media of old animals contracts less in response to norepinephrine. Although this may suggest a reduced receptor density, it may result from an increased stiffness of the tunica media of the vessel as the content of connective tissue increases.

## Aging Changes in Homeostatic Regulation

In chapter 5, the reduced sensitivity of the baroreceptor reflex was mentioned. In many old people, this produces significant orthostatic hypotension, since neither the peripheral resistance nor the heart rate responds adequately to the challenge of venous pooling that occurs on standing. In some old persons, the cardiovascular regulation may not be able to maintain the arterial pressure when muscle vasculature is dilated by exercise or by the administration of nitroprusside. Performance of the Valsalva maneuver by old individuals produces a greater decrease in pressure during the straining phase than in a young adult, and on release of the intrathoracic pressure, there is no rebound to the elevated pressure. Fainting as a consequence of coughing or straining to urinate is a reflection of this same impaired regulation.

## Aging of Homeostatic Mechanisms

### Thermoregulation

Maintenance of a constant internal temperature in the body depends on the integrity of a feedback system involving receptors, central control elements, and effector systems. Homeothermy calls for a balance between heat gain and heat loss. The mechanisms involved are shown as follows:

| HEAT GAIN | HEAT LOSS |
|---|---|
| Basal heat production | Radiation |
| Heat production by | Conduction |
| muscular activity | Convection |
| Radiation | Evaporation of water |
| Conduction | (either insensible or |
| Convection | by sweating) |

The rates of heat exchange by physical means, radiation, conduction, and convection depend on the surface area available for exchange and the temperature gradient between the body surface and the environment. Basal heat production is determined by the mass of actively metabolizing tissue. Heat production above the basal level is determined by the amount of activity and the mass of muscle available for activity. Evaporative heat loss comes about by the transpiration of water vapor across the skin, by loss of water from the moist respiratory surfaces, and by sweating.

The core temperature of the body is regulated by control of metabolic heat production, by control of the surface temperature (i.e., skin temperature), and by control of evaporative cooling.

The body modifies skin temperature either by delivering large volumes of warm blood to the superficial vessels of the skin or by retaining the warm blood below the insulation afforded by subcutaneous adipose tissue and constricted cutaneous blood vessels.

The following elements of the heat balance sheet change with age.

1. The amount of active tissue mass per unit of surface area is less in the old than in the young.
2. The capability for activity is generally less.
3. Thinning of the skin and loss of subcutaneous fat reduce the insulating power of the integument.
4. Sweat glands atrophy with age. Sweating, which is the most effective route of heat dissipation, is therefore less available.
5. Skin circulation is reduced, especially in the extremities, as a compensatory response to reduced cardiac output.

As a consequence, the old person is less able to cope with the challenge of either an increased need for heat loss or an increased need for heat production and conservation.

## Basal Body Temperature

The resting body temperature measured in a comfortable environment shows no significant change with age. Skin temperatures of the hands and feet in particular are lower in the old, however, reflecting the poor circulation to these areas.

## Thermal Sensitivity and Comfort

Although it is often thought that old persons prefer environments that are warmer than those identified as comfortable by the young, there is little evidence to support this. In one study, older subjects regarded as "slightly warm" ambient temperatures several degrees lower than those so identified by younger people. Another study demonstrated that older people were not uncomfortable at temperatures that produced a net heat loss. This lesser sensitivity to cold means that individuals are less likely to take appropriate action to maintain their body temperature—for example, putting on a sweater or increasing physical activity. At the other end of the thermal scale, old people report as "too warm" environments that are comfortable to the young.

## Central Control Sensitivity

The efficiency of the central control elements can be judged by how promptly the mechanisms of heat gain or loss are engaged when the need arises. When exposed to cold, old people shiver to increase heat production later than young people, although once recruited, the increased metabolic heat production is equally great. When exposed to an increased heat load, old people show a delayed onset of the sweating response. After sweating is established in the old, it continues longer after exposure to the load— a result of the low rate of sweating and therefore of heat dissipation. These observations suggest that the target temperature of thermoregulation is not affected by age but that the precision of the control has been lost; a greater "error" must be present to initiate the appropriate correction.

## Hyperthermia and Hypothermia

The changes that have been described make the old especially susceptible to thermal damage. The frequency of death from hyperthermia increases greatly in those over age 60. The effect of elevated temperatures is cumulative, with the number of incidents of hyperthermia increasing, for example, as a spell of hot weather continues. Much of this progressive morbidity may be accounted for by the failure to maintain a water and salt balance in persons unable to fend for themselves. When the body temperature reaches 41 C, central depression of regulation occurs. The elevated temperature stimulates metabolism and heat production. A positive feedback loop is established and death, usually from respiratory depression, results when the body temperature reaches 43 to 44 C.

Depression of the sense of cold discomfort, inability to increase physical activity or to "micro-climatize" against the cold, and low basal heat production and poor insulation make a cold environment a special threat to the old. Only relatively recently has the magnitude of the problem of "accidental hypothermia" been appreciated. Studies in the United Kingdom have estimated that 10% of old people might be susceptible. In a sample of old people admitted to the hospital (for reasons other than hypothermia), 3.5% were found to be hypothermic as judged by a body temperature recorded in freshly voided urine of cooler than 35 C. A survey in this country suggested that 25,000 people may have suffered a bout of hypothermia in 1975. Impaired mechanisms of heat production and conservation allow the body temperature to fall to 35 C. At this point, central control mechanisms are depressed. A positive feedback loop is established, with the falling temperature further depressing metabolism and heat production. As the temperature continues to fall, the myocardium is depressed and sinus bradycardia ensues. With further decrease, arrhythmias occur, leading finally to ventricular fibrillation. In addition to age, other risk factors are the tricyclic antidepressants, which impair thermoregulation; alcohol, which produces a paralytic cutaneous vasodilation; inadequately heated rooms, especially bedrooms and bathrooms; and inadequate diet. Of individuals whose temperature falls into the range of 32 to 35 C, 35% die. Severe hypothermia with temperatures of 28 C kills 65% to 80% of those afflicted.

The kidney function is also impaired as the body cools and the "cold diuresis" that results imposes the further hazard of dehydration.

## Acid-Base Balance

The pH of the blood is affected very little by age and, as is general in the aging homeostatic systems, it is only when challenge is offered that impaired regulation is seen. Three processes are fundamental to acid-base regulation: (1) buffering of the load of acid or base, (2) adjustment of the pH toward normal by respiratory modifications, and (3) renal elimination of the excess acid or base.

Buffering of a load of noncarbonic acid is initially rapid using bicarbonate of plasma and interstitial fluid, then slower using the proton acceptor capacity of intracellular protein, and still slower using the buffering power of the bone. The total buffer capacity of the old person is less than that of the young. The interstitial fluid volume per unit of body weight is lower, and the bicarbonate concentration is slightly lower. The reduced lean tissue mass per unit of body weight and the loss of bone mineral both reduce the available tissue buffering.

The rapid phase of buffering of a strong acid produces carbonic acid, which can readily be eliminated by the lungs. Although the old person has diminished respiratory reserve and some reduction of diffusing capacity at the alveolar membrane, the effect on carbon dioxide elimination is negligible. The high solubility of carbon dioxide and the consequent high diffusibility provide a wide safety margin. Only when a gross challenge calls for an extreme ventilatory response is an age-related deficiency seen.

The third stage of regulation, which restores the buffer systems to their normal state, is performed by the kidney. In a young person, this correction requires hours or even days. The role of the kidney is threefold. First, it regulates the quantity of bicarbonate that is reabsorbed or allowed to escape into the urine. The response to an acid load is to maximize this recovery. Second, the kidney eliminates hydrogen ion by means of the buffers presented to the distal tubule. Third, the kidney regenerates buffer base by replacing the urinary cation by the ammonium ion.

The reduced effective mass of the kidney clearly hinders all three functions. A reduced rate of formation of glomerular filtrate leads to a reduced presentation of bicarbonate to the proximal tubule. In the case of an acid load, this is not important since the object is to maximize the recovery of bicarbonate. On the other hand, if the disturbance of the acid-base balance calls for the elimination of excess bicarbonate, the process is necessarily slow since only the amount filtered per unit time can be excreted.

The low glomerular filtration rate leads to a reduced delivery of buffers to the distal nephron, where the titratable acidity of the urine is generated. Since only a limited gradient of pH can be generated, a reduction in the total quantity of the buffer limits the elimination of $H^+$ ion. A little compensation for the lower glomerular filtration of buffers is afforded by the decreased reabsorption of phosphate in the old kidney. The magnitude of this change is trivial in the net, however.

The old kidney has a reduced ability to deaminate glutamine to provide "new" urinary cations. The ammonia that enters the distal tubule fluid also serves to trap hydrogen ion and carry it out into the urine. When the acid-base regulation is tested by the administration of oral ammonium chloride, the rate of elimination of the resulting load of hydrochloric acid in the old person is only one third of that in the young adult.

## Volume and Tonicity of Body Fluids

Homeostasis of the volume and tonicity of the body fluids calls for precise regulation of the body content of water and salt. Under most circumstances, the intakes of water and salt exceed the minimal requirements, and regulation of the body content is essentially through excretion by the kidney. Under some circumstances, other routes of water and salt loss may become quantitatively more important than the kidney. Heavy sweating under conditions of heat load and loss of fluid from the gut in diarrhea are examples of special circumstances where the kidney plays a role in conservation.

The efficiency of the renal regulation of water and salt balance may be judged by how promptly and precisely loads of water or salt are eliminated or, on the other hand, conserved when needed. The renal operation of elimination or conservation involves the integrity of the hypothalamo-hypophyseal axis for vasopressin secretion and of the aldosterone system of the adrenal cortex.

The system for vasopressin secretion and liberation does not appear to be affected by age; in fact, under conditions of dehydration, circulating levels of vasopressin may be significantly higher in the old than in young adults. Circulating levels of aldosterone are lower in old people, and the zona glomerulosa is less responsive to both local direct stimulation and control by the renin-angiotensin system.

Basic to overall regulation is the need for adequate volumes of glomerular filtrate upon which the endocrine-governed tubular processes can operate. When the rates of glomerular filtration are lower, the absolute quantities of water or salt that can be eliminated or conserved per unit of time are reduced, even when the tubular processes retain their efficiency. However, the efficiency of the tubular processes is not retained, especially in regard to water. The medulla of the old kidney has less osmotic stratification, and furthermore, the distal tubules and collecting ducts become less responsive to vasopressin. Vasopressin action at these sites involves cAMP (cyclic adenosine monophosphate) as the second messenger, and this may be an example of a general reduced activity of adenyl cyclase in aging. Although in the young adult, maximal water conservation can lead to the production of urine that is four times as concentrated as plasma, in the old, this ratio falls to less than three. The elimination of solute loads in the old is thus expensive in terms of absolute volumes of water lost and slow because of low filtration. When the challenge is to eliminate excess water, the deficiency of the old kidney is seen in the diluting operation. In the young person, urine can be formed that is less than one-tenth as concentrated as plasma. Impaired salt recovery in the old kidney shifts the minimal osmotic concentration of urine closer to that of plasma. Excretion of a water load is thus slow (low glomerular filtration) and expensive of salt. Given adequate time to restore balance, the old individual performs adequately, but the slow rates of elimination or conservation tend to produce larger, longer sustained shifts from the target position.

Although the intake of water and salt normally exceeds minimal requirements, intake usually involves a voluntary response to the sensations of thirst and appetite. There is no evidence that the primary sensation of thirst in the old is lessened, but they may have physical problems in obtaining and drinking fluids. The acuity of taste for salt is reduced in the old, thus they tend to increase their salt intake in an effort to satisfy their taste. The danger for old people is thus dehydration and hyperosmolarity rather than salt depletion and hypoosmolarity. It is especially important to bear in mind the slower regulation of volume and tonicity in the older person when fluids are administered parenterally or when diuretics, which may severely challenge the water and solute balance of the body, are prescribed.

## SUGGESTED READING

Besdine R.W.: Accidental hypothermia: The body's energy crisis. *Geriatrics* 34(12):51–59, 1979.

Fox R.H., MacGibbon R., Davies L., et al.: Problems of the old and the cold. *Br. Med. J.* 1:21–24, 1973.

Frolkis V.V.: Regulatory processes in the mechanism of aging. *Exp. Gerontol.* 3:113–123, 1968.

Hellon R.F., Lind A.R., Weiner J.S.: The physiological reactions of men of two age groups to a hot environment. *J. Physiol.* 133:118–131, 1956.

Minnaker K., Rowe J., Sparrow D.: Impaired cardiovascular adaptation to vasodilation in the elderly. *Gerontologist* 20:163, 1981.

Norris A.H., Shoek N.W., Yiengst M.J.: Age changes in heart rate and blood pressure responses to tilting and standardized exercises. *Circulation* 8:521–526, 1953.

Wagner J.A., Robinson S., Marino R.P.: Age and temperature regulation of humans in neutral and cold environments. *J. Appl. Physiol.* 37:562–565, 1974.

Wollner L., Spalding J.M.K.: The autonomic nervous system, in Brocklehurst J.C. (ed.): *Geriatric Medicine and Gerontology*. Edinburgh, Churchill Livingstone, 1973, pp. 235–253.

# PART III

# OTHER CONSEQUENCES OF AGING

# 10 / Aging Changes in Higher Functions

NOWHERE IS IT more difficult than in the brain to separate the eugeric changes of normal aging from disease processes. The changes that are regarded as part of normal aging—for example, loss of neurons, alterations in the metabolism of neurotransmitters, and the development of plaques and neurofibrillary inclusions— differ only in a quantitative way from the signs of brain disease. Likewise, the changes in cortical function that are regarded as eugeric may well be part of a continuum that has dementia as its extreme. If this concept is valid, then the reduction of intellectual function displayed by some old people and presently regarded as normal may in fact be either prevented or delayed once we have a sufficient understanding of the interplay of genetic, cardiovascular, and environmental factors in the cause of brain disease.

## The Aging EEG

Major alterations occur in the electric activity of the cortex as a consequence of cerebral atrophy or vascular disease. It is therefore difficult to identify alterations that may properly be described as normal aging. It is generally agreed, however, that a slowing of the alpha rhythm is typical of the healthy older person. In the young individual, the rhythm has a dominant frequency of approximately 10 Hz; in older persons, there is a downward shift to the range of 8 to 9.5 Hz. Within this lower range, the lowest values are seen in the oldest individuals. One study has shown that in two age-matched groups, one of "good learners" and one of "poor learners," the latter showed a lower dominant frequency. During middle age, there is an increase in fast activity in the 12- to 30-Hz frequency and this diminishes with aging. The loss is marked in individuals who have significant mental deterioration. The continued presence of fast activity in the older person is regarded as a good sign. There is increased slow activity of the delta and theta frequencies, which, in the normal person, tends to be focal rather than diffuse. The temporal area is a favored site for this activity, but there is no known clinical correlate of this change. Measures of learning, memory, and IQ do not differ in groups that show or do not show this activity. When studied longitudinally, subjects who showed foci of slow activity had more loss of verbal function. Diffuse slow activity involving large cortical areas is associated with severe mental impairment.

### Averaged Evoked Potentials (AEP)

AEPs are potentials recorded from the scalp following the presentation of a stimulus—visual, auditory, or tactile. The potentials are evoked by a series of stimuli presented one or two seconds apart and are averaged by computer. In this process of averaging, the potentials that are time-locked to the presentation of the stimulus are enhanced and the "noise" or non-time-locked activity diminishes. Records take the form of a series of negative and positive deflections during the 500 or 600 msec following the stimulus. The early events of the evoked response are usually taken to reflect the transmission of information within the nervous system, whereas those that occur later are generally related to processing and storage. Records are analyzed in terms of both the latency (time from the stimulus presentation) of a particular positive or negative wave and the amplitude. When the responses of old and young subjects are compared, differences are seen in both features. Latencies of early wave forms are increased and there is also an increase in amplitude. These differences occur whether the stimulus is visual or tactile. When individuals with chronic brain syndromes are compared with age-matched controls, the major change is in the later events of the AEP, where latencies are increased and the wave forms attenuated. Similar changes are seen in delirium and during sleep.

The increased latency in healthy old persons could arise from a slowing of the transmission in peripheral elements. If this were the case, then one might expect the stimulus to be dispersed in time. (Compare this with the dispersion seen in the EMG of old subjects, where polyphasic potentials are common.) One would expect the amplitudes of the wave forms to be reduced. Since amplitudes typically increase, the difference between young and old probably resides centrally. When we consider that age is associated with a reduction in the numbers of cortical neurons, the explanation of the phenomenon may be that in the aged there is greater synchrony of discharge of the neurons, perhaps resulting from fewer competing channels of information. An alternative explanation may be that in the aged cortex there is less inhibitory input. The changed latencies may be a direct reflection of impaired membrane processes of depolarization and repolarization.

### Sleep

Sleep studies of young and elderly persons have revealed the following:

1. Older persons take longer to fall asleep than do the young.
2. Total time spent asleep is not different between the groups.
3. Old persons awaken more frequently during the night and spend a longer time awake on each occasion. The older person thus spends longer total time in bed (Fig 10–1).
4. The transition between sleep and wakefulness is abrupt in old people in contrast with the period of "coming to the surface" that young people go through. Old people are thus considered "light sleepers."

The pattern of sleep is conveniently described in terms of the EEG pattern and the presence or absence of rapid eye movements. Sleep is thus divided into slow-wave sleep (SSW) and sleep

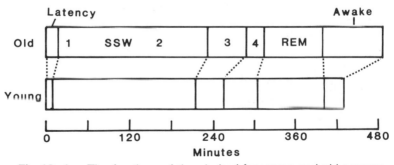

**Fig 10–1.**—The fractions of time in bed for young and old persons. Numbers refer to the phases of slow-wave sleep (SSW). (Based on data from Feinberg I.: in Terry R.D., Gershon S. [eds.]: *Neurobiology of Aging,* New York, Raven Press, 1976, pp. 23–41.)

accompanied by rapid eye movements (SREM). SSW can be divided into stages on the basis of the dominant EEG pattern. The transition from the waking state to sleep is marked by the appearance of irregular fast activity of low amplitude. This is stage 1 of slow-wave sleep and is usually of short duration.

Stage 2 is characterized by low-amplitude, slow-wave forms. "Sleep spindles" may appear in which the amplitude waxes and wanes.

Stage 3 typically shows the features of stage 2 with the addition of high-voltage delta rhythm occupying half or less of the period under study.

Stage 4 is dominated by high-voltage delta activity. This is the deepest sleep in terms of the level of stimulus needed for arousal. It is most common in the early part of sleep and occurs less frequently as the night progresses. An association has been suggested between stage 4 SSW and the "metabolic repair" of the waking period. The EEG during SREM is typically irregular and of low voltage; there are no sleep spindles. In the elderly, the time occupied by stage 4 sleep is about half of the young value, but there is a compensatory increase in the amount of stage 3 sleep. It appears that in the elderly, the high-voltage delta activity that is the criterion for these stages becomes more diffusely distributed among lower-amplitude activity. In both young and old persons, the sum of the durations of stages 3 and 4 remains close to 20% of the sleeping time.

Sleep spindles occur less frequently in the old, and they are of a lower frequency and amplitude. A similar depression of spindle activity is seen in young hypothyroid individuals. In these cases, adequate replacement therapy normalizes the pattern.

SREM shows only a slight reduction with age, but the pattern of appearance of this phase changes. In young people, the early bouts of SREM are short and they lengthen progressively during the night. In the old, the first bout of SREM is significantly longer than subsequent ones.

No correlation has been made between sleep pattern and brain function, although hypotheses have been offered. One, for example, proposes that the phases of sleep reflect stages in the metabolic activity of the brain that are essentially complementary to the waking information-processing functions.

## Dreaming

When a young person is awakened during a period of SREM sleep, dreams can regularly be recalled; dream recall is rare in the person who wakes during SSW. This observation has led to the identification of SREM as "dreaming sleep." The time in which dreams can be recalled is limited. If awakening is delayed more than a few minutes after the end of SREM, no recall is possible. This suggests that waking at the end of SREM is necessary for consolidation of the memory. The major change that occurs with aging is a sharp reduction in dream recall even when the person is awakened immediately after SREM. One study of dream content has suggested that the old dreamer plays a more passive role than the young.

Penile erections are also temporally related to periods of SREM sleep. In young men, erections accompany about 80% of the periods of SREM sleep. In old men, although there is considerable individual variation, the average frequency of erection is only half that seen in the young. The erections of older men are also less complete.

## Memory and Learning

The stereotype of the aged person is one who is slow to learn, has a poor short-term memory, but has good recall for remote events—long-term memory. Memory and learning are difficult to separate. Learning may be defined as an alteration in behavior as a result of experience, whereas memory involves the recall of experience or recognition. Since one remembers what is learned, these two functions are probably facets of the same process. The division of memory into two parts, one for recent events and one for more remote, arises from the way in which memory is tested and from the present models of memory formation. One such model is shown in Figure 10–2.

Essentially, sensory information is taken into storage, where it is held briefly. A process then makes an abstract of the salient features of the information and the abstract goes into short-term memory. A second process forms a permanent trace, or engram, of the information, which is laid down in long-term memory. Information in these memories can be used in either of two ways. It

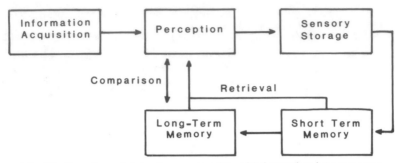

**Fig 10-2.**—A model for the processing of information into memory.

may be recalled and perceived, or it may be used as a comparative template to recognize an object, word, or experience. For memory to occur, information must first be acquired. Impairment of the senses in older persons is thus a prime factor in their decreased ability to remember and learn.

Evidence from animal experiments has suggested two fundamental memory processes, one a facilitation at cholinergic synapses and one involving RNA and the synthesis of a variety of memory-specific peptides. As mentioned in chapter 7, major age-related changes occur in cholinergic neurotransmitter synthesis and disposal and likewise there appears to be some impairment of protein synthesis with aging.

Short-term memory is often tested by a person's ability to repeat a list of digits read aloud or presented visually. The repetition may be either immediate or delayed for seconds or minutes. Such tests show no aging effect into middle age and thereafter a small but significant decline in results. When recall is delayed, the difference between old and young becomes greater. Another test, this one of recognition memory, involves the presentation of a list of words. The list is then taken away and the subject is asked to recognize the words in a second longer list. This test reveals a decline beginning in the 30s and reaching a plateau in the 60s and 70s. When long-term memory is tested by recall of historical events, men perform better than women. Information that has a high personal impact is better recalled than neutral information. In general, experiments have not shown that ease of recall increases as the length of time of the material in memory increases.

Experiments that test learning often take the form of association of word pairs. The task is learning the "response" word to match a "stimulus" word. There is little difference between old and young individuals provided the pacing of learning is slow. If the association is tested in reverse, however—the subject is asked to provide the stimulus word when presented with the response— old subjects perform poorly. This is interpreted as showing an impairment of peripheral learning—that is, learning what is an incidental rather than a primary task. One often hears that old people tend to become "single-minded" at a task and ignore what is going on about them. This comment is often pejorative. In a young person, this behavior would be called "concentration."

Research is being done on improving memory function in the old via the restoration of adequate concentrations of acetylcholine in the brain. One line of this work promotes the increased intake of choline in the form of lecithin. An interesting recent observation is that short-term memory can be improved by the intranasal administration of arginine-vasopressin, the antidiuretic hormone.

Another higher function that is often tested is psychomotor speed, in which a relatively simple repetitive task must be carried out as swiftly as possible. The test may take the form of copying a page of digits or crossing out a series of horizontal lines. Older subjects perform poorly on these tests whether they call for some or no cognitive skill. The decline in function begins at approximately age 40 and is rapid. The 70-year-old completes only about half as many items as does the 30-year-old. A related test calls for the subject to write as slowly as possible. Young men but not young women have this skill. Again, there is a very sharp decrease in performance with age. It appears that the older individual operates within a fixed and narrow range of speed in performing tasks. The failure to accelerate may be a deliberate attempt to avoid error in the presence of impaired cognition; the inability to perform more slowly than is customary may reflect a loss of cortical inhibition in the old person.

### SUGGESTED READING

Botwinick J.: *Aging and Behavior: A Comprehensive Integration of Research Findings*. New York, Springer Publishing Co., 1973.
Botwinick J., Storandt M.: *Memory, Related Functions and Age*. Springfield, Ill.: Charles C Thomas, Publisher, 1974.
Feinberg, I.: Changes in sleep cycle patterns with age. *J. Psychiatr. Res.* 10:283–306, 1974.

Kales J.D.: Aging and sleep, in Goldman R., Rockstein M. (eds.): *The Physiology and Pathology of Human Aging*. New York, Academic Press, 1975, pp. 187–202.

Kent S.: Can drugs halt memory loss? *Geriatrics* 36(2):34–41, 1981.

Thompson L.W., Marsh G.P.: Psychophysiological studies of aging, in Eisdorfer C., Lawton M.P. (eds.): *The Psychology of Adult Development and Aging*. Washington, D.C., American Psychological Association, 1973, pp. 112–148.

# 11 / Nutrition, Drugs, and Biologic Age

## Nutrition in Aging

In laboratory animals, restriction of caloric intake extends the maturation period and the life span. On the other hand, the chronically undernourished man in India, for example, who does not enjoy the laboratory animal's protection from disease, has a life span substantially shorter than that of an individual in the West or in Japan. Malnutrition is present, nonetheless, in all age groups in this country. It takes the forms of a lack of specific nutrients and also overnutrition and its consequent obesity. The latter arises in large part from a diet high in "convenience foods" and empty calories.

Food becomes less attractive to the older person for several reasons. Loss of the senses of smell and taste robs food of much of its pleasure. The age-related changes in esophageal motility and competence of the lower esophageal sphincter can make mealtimes uncomfortable. Especially for the older person living alone, the chore of shopping and cooking seems hardly worthwhile, and less nutritious, prepared foods such as TV dinners are substituted. Loss of teeth without adequate replacement makes chewing difficult, and this together with a reduced flow of saliva leads the older person to select soft foods, often carbohydrates, rather than the more demanding meats, fresh vegetables, and salads. Too often the cost of a well-balanced, nutritious diet is prohibitive to the older person.

The first criterion for an adequate diet is that it provides enough calories to support the body's metabolism without producing obesity. It is important to consider two facets of metabolism separately. First is the basal metabolic rate, which falls progressively with age after full growth has been achieved and reflects the slow reduction in lean body mass. The second facet is the calories needed to support activity. With aging, and especially with unemployment, there is likely to be a substantial decrease in physical activity (Fig

**109**

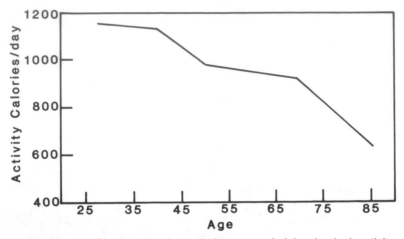

**Fig 11–1.**—Changes in the calories expended in physical activity based on self-reported diaries. Note the biphasic nature of the fall in activity—an early fall as energetic leisure activities are reduced and a later fall during retirement.

11–1). The requirement for "activity calories" differs widely from one individual to another. Although there are tables that specify the energy cost of everyday tasks and leisure activities, these are an imperfect basis with which to assess the calorie requirements of old people; with age, the "machinery of work" becomes less efficient largely because of the stiffening of joints, the increased internal work involved in muscle contraction, and impaired muscular coordination. This lowered efficiency is more marked as the work that is undertaken becomes more strenuous. In general, an old person has a decreased calorie requirement. The advice is often given that intake should be reduced by 15% from ages 45 to 65 and thereafter by 10% each decade.

Protein requirement estimated on the basis of lean body mass does not alter with age, and inadequate intake is common. This can easily occur in an old person who continues to eat the same dietary mix as when young. The person may merely reduce total intake to match the reduced calorie requirement instead of increasing the quality of the diet so that a greater fraction of total calories comes from protein. As mentioned, both physiological and economic factors work against such improvement of the diet. Some old persons absorb less fat due to inadequate secretion of pancreatic lipase. Although fats are important to make the diet more palatable and as a vehicle for the essential fatty acids and fat-soluble vitamins, the older person should reduce total fat intake so that no more than 25% of calories come from this source.

There is general agreement that the requirements of older people for vitamins are the same as those of the young except for thiamine and vitamin A, of which some authorities recommend a 30% increase in intake. Adequate intake is, of course, dependent on the quality of the diet. Analysis of the typical diets of old people suggests that in general requirements are met, but there is a reduced margin of safety so that deficiencies can more easily arise when the old person is sick or disabled. Common problems are inadequate amounts of meat in the diet, which may lead to a deficiency of B-group vitamins (especially $B_{12}$), an inadequate intake of fruits and vegetables, and a deficiency of vitamin C. In the old person confined to the house, synthesis of vitamin D in the skin is reduced and a deficiency may arise, especially in those who avoid fats. The aging loss of kidney mass reduces the formation of the active form of the vitamin, and as a consequence, there is less efficient absorption of calcium in the gut. When the old person's diet consists of convenience foods, vitamin supplementation may be indicated, but there is no rationale for the massive vitamin supplementation sometimes proposed.

Of the minerals, deficiencies of calcium and iron are most common with age, since changes in the absorption of these elements may reduce their availability to marginal levels. In this country, the recommended daily allowance of calcium for persons older than 50 is 800 mg compared with 500 mg for younger adults. Stores of iron in the bone marrow of old people tend to be low, so that a small loss of blood may produce anemia. Reduced gastric acidity is a major factor in impaired iron absorption.

The fiber content of the diet is valuable in maintaining gut motility and preventing constipation (provided fluid intake is maintained). Excessive intake of fiber, however, can prevent the adequate absorption of essential nutrients including the trace elements. Fiber can be obtained from fruits, vegetables, and cereal products, which should be conspicuous parts of the diet.

In general, the diet of the old person should match that of the younger adult except for being stripped of empty calories (e.g., confectionaries and alcohol) and reinforced with milk and milk products.

## Drugs and the Aged

Old people consume more prescription and over-the-counter drugs per capita than do young people. In the late 1970s, 25% of all drug sales were to the oldest 11% of the population. The incidence of adverse reactions to drugs (per drug taken) is twice as high in the old as in the young. In part, this may be due to interactions between multiple drugs being taken for multiple diseases, but these adverse reactions may also arise from the altered physiology of the old. The action of drugs may be considered in two major ways. One is the kinetics of the drug in terms of its absorption, transport, distribution, metabolism (biotransformation), and elimination. The other aspect of drug action is the so-called pharmacodynamics—the interaction of the drug with a receptor site, through which its effect on the target cell is produced.

### Absorption
In old persons, reduced blood flow to the gut, changes in the absorptive epithelium, reduced motility, and delayed gastric emptying all alter drug absorption. A reduction in the acidity of gastric contents, which is a small change in the absence of atrophic gastritis and largely confined to men, affects the solubility and ionization of some drugs.

### Transport in the Blood
The extent to which a drug is free to distribute throughout the body components is dependent on the extent to which it is bound to plasma protein and red blood cells. The concentration of plasma albumin is lower in the old; hence, more drugs that are normally bound to albumin are in the free, available form. In general, the binding of drugs to red blood cells does not change with age. This makes sense because red blood cells are constantly replaced and thus do not reflect the age of the individual.

These two factors, absorption and transport, are the primary determinants of the quantity of drugs available to the body. Drug effects are dependent on concentration and the time the drug is present (the area under the curve of concentration plotted against time). A useful characterization of the pharmacokinetics is the half-life $(t^{1/2})$ of the drug within the body compartments:

$$t^{1/2} = 0.693 \times \frac{\text{Volume of distribution}}{\text{Clearance}}$$

### Volume of Distribution

With age, the total amount of body water becomes a smaller fraction of the body weight, so that drugs that distribute in total body water become relatively more concentrated if administered on a body weight basis. Also, the increased body fat content of the older person leads to the accumulation and extended presence of drugs that are very soluble in lipids.

### Clearance

Clearance of a drug refers to two basic processes: (1) the *biotransformation* of the drug into an active or inactive product and (2) the elimination of the drug from the body.

The process of biotransformation commonly occurs in the liver and involves the microsomal enzyme systems for hydrolysis, oxidation, or conjugation of the drug. The reduction in liver mass and blood flow with age slows this process. In addition, with age the microsomal enzyme systems are less readily induced.

Drugs are eliminated from the body by the gut (sometimes following hepatic secretion into the bile), by the skin in sweat, by the lungs if volatile, or by the kidney. Of these routes, the last is the major avenue for most drugs. The decrease in the number of nephrons with the associated reduction in the glomerular filtration rate and renal perfusion leads to a persistence within the body of drugs that are simply filtered or that are also actively secreted by the tubular epithelium. The age-related reduction in the ability to concentrate the urine or to excrete osmotically uncommitted ("free") water may also be a pertinent factor in drug elimination.

Glomerular filtration is commonly evaluated by the clearance of creatinine and the absolute rate of creatinine excretion correlates with the lean body mass. Attempts have been made to index the optimal dose of drugs to either or both of these measurements. Although such an index might be imperfect, it would be superior to schedules of administration based on body weight or surface area.

Volatile drugs eliminated by the lungs are retained longer in the old body as a consequence of the increased functional residual capacity (i.e., reduced ventilatory coefficient) and the poorer matching of ventilation and perfusion.

## Interaction with Target Tissues

The activity of many drugs changes with age independent of the amount of the drug in the target tissue. These changes may be due to (1) alterations in the interaction between the drug and the receptor sites or (2) limitations in the responsiveness of the target tissue.

In a young person, atropine produces a large increase in heart rate (as much as 50% of the initial rate); in the old, the rate change is trivial. This may be explained by the reduced number of cholinergic receptors in old hearts. In general, the old have less response to drugs that have a stimulant effect on the CNS (e.g., amphetamine) but more response to CNS depressants (e.g., chlorpromazine). Barbiturates, which are depressants in the young, tend to be stimulants in the old—an effect explained by differential aging of the target centers (possibly differential loss of receptor sites). In experimental animals, sensitivity to alloxan increases with age. In old animals, the number of islet cells is reduced and, hence, the effective load of alloxan per cell (or per receptor site) is increased. An example of the limitation of response at the target tissue is the reaction of the aortic smooth muscle to norepinephrine. With aging, the aorta becomes less compliant (stiffer) and the contractile response is reduced. For this reason, the relaxation response of the vessel to isoproterenol is much reduced in the old.

The β-blocking agent propranolol reduces cardiac output, but in the old, the change is lessened in proportion with the lower initial output.

Clearly, the use of drugs in the aged calls for special caution. The regimen must recognize the changed dynamics and kinetics of the drug. For the old person living alone, further danger arises from failing vision, loss of memory, and confusion. Because of poor eyesight, the wrong drug may be taken, poor short-term memory may lead the individual to duplicate a dose, and the signs of any adverse reaction may not be recognized.

## Biologic Age

Typical of the changes in the physiology of aging individuals is a variation in the rate at which they occur. The idea of "biologic age" has been applied extensively in the study of growth and development, where well-defined end points of the stages of maturation—progress of calcification, eruption of teeth, and onset of puberty, for example—are available. Aging, on the other hand, is a continuous process with few such end points. Nonetheless, extension of the concept of biologic or physiological age to older individuals is important for three reasons. First, such a measure would serve as a tool in determining the effectiveness of an intervention designed to delay aging (incorporation of antioxidants in the diet, for example). Second, it would guide in identifying environmental factors that accelerate aging. Third, it would be important to industry and to society in general where the use of chronological age to determine a person's employment status or certain benefits ignores the wide individual variation in physical and mental capabilities.

Attempts have been made to develop a battery of measurements to be used for estimating physiological age. Tests selected for such a battery would ideally meet the following criteria:

1. The function tested should show a marked change with age so that there is significant alteration over a reasonably short span of years—for example, three to five years.
2. The tests chosen should cover as broad a spectrum of functional systems as possible.
3. The tests should be performed with as little disturbance of the subject as possible.
4. The performance of the test should not be dependent on the motivation of the subject.
5. The tests should be suitable for screening large numbers of people.

It has become apparent that most aging changes begin at early middle age—40 to 50 years. Thus, it is probably futile to attempt to develop a battery of tests that cover the span from young adulthood to extreme old age; it is more profitable to consider particularly the years from age 40 onward. A battery of tests was developed by Hollingsworth and his colleagues in 1965 for examining

TABLE 11–1. — MEASURES OF BIOLOGIC AGE

| VARIABLE | CORRELATION WITH AGE |
|---|---|
| 1. Skin deformability | +0.604 |
| 2. Systolic blood pressure | +0.519 |
| 3. Vital capacity | −0.402 |
| 4. Hand grip strength | −0.323 |
| 5. Reaction time | +0.488 |
| 6. Vibratory sensitivity | −0.537 |
| 7. Visual acuity | −0.423 |
| 8. Threshold of hearing at 4,000 Hz | −0.596 |
| 9. Level of serum cholesterol | +0.234 |

the survivors in Hiroshima. Nine functions were selected. These are listed in Table 11–1 together with the correlation of the function with age. Hollingsworth studied more than 400 individuals and found a high degree of correlation between chronological age and an index of physiologic age derived from these measurements.

Borkan and Norris (1980) published a procedure for the assessment of biologic age that uses a similar battery of tests. They used data from the longitudinal study conducted by the National Institute on Aging. Having established the regression of a particular measurement on age, they subtracted the predicted value for that measurement from that observed in an individual and then converted the residual to a $z$-score. The $z$-scores, either positive (arbitrarily taken as indicating a biologic age greater than chronological) or negative, were then plotted as a profile. Such a profile might show that a person is younger than his years in, say, cardiovascular function but has "overaged" in psychomotor function.

It is interesting to note that graying of the hair and the radiographic density of the metacarpals correlate with age even better than any of the functional measures reported ($r > 0.70$). The quantitation of the first is tedious, involving establishing the percent of gray hairs in an axillary sample. Measurement of radiographic density cannot conveniently be included in rapid surveys of large numbers of individuals. It is for these reasons that they do not appear in the test batteries. Timed force expiratory volume also has an excellent correlation with age when tested in highly motivated and experienced subjects but not in a casual examination.

The potential value of biologic age in understanding and treating the problems of the older individual is great.

## SUGGESTED READING

### NUTRITION

Exton-Smith A.N., Caird F.I. (eds.): *Metabolic and Nutritional Disorders in the Elderly*. Chicago, Year Book Medical Publishers, 1980.
Harper A.E.: Dietary guidelines for the elderly. *Geriatrics* 36(7):34–43, 1981.
Rockstein M., Sussman M.L.: *Nutrition, Longevity and Aging*. New York, Academic Press, 1976.

### DRUGS

Jarvick L.F., Greenblatt M.D., Harman D.: *Clinical Pharmacology and the Aging Patient*. New York, Raven Press, 1981.
Krupka L.R., Vener A.M.: Hazards of drug use among the elderly. *Gerontologist* 19(1):90–95, 1979.

### BIOLOGIC AGE

Comfort A.: *Biology of Senescence*. New York, Elsevier North-Holland, Inc., 1979, pp. 299–312.
Hollingsworth J.W., Hashizume A., Jablon S.: Correlations between tests of aging in Hiroshima subjects—an attempt to define "physiologic age." *Yale J. Biol. Med.* 38:11–26, 1965.
Borkan G.A., Norris A.H.: Assessment of biological age using a profile of physical parameters. *J. Gerontol.* 35:177, 1980.

## Postscript

A man isn't old when his hair turns grey
When his figure stoops and his teeth decay,
But he's surely headed for that last deep sleep
When his mind makes dates which his body can't keep

Anon.

# Index

## A

A-a$_{O2}$ difference, 47
Abdominal reflexes: superficial, 70
Absorption: and alimentary tract, 63
Acclimatization: to high temperatures or high altitudes, 11–12
Accommodation, 72
  age-related alteration in, 73
Acetylcholine, 69, 107
Acetylcholinesterase, 91
Acid
  -base
    balance, 94–96
    homeostasis, 60
    secretion, resting, 62
Acidity: titratable, 59, 95
ACTH, 81
Action potentials: polyphasic, 68
Adaptation: dark, 74
Adenosine
  diphosphate, ATP:ADP ratio, 36
  monophosphate, 16
    cAMP:cGMP ratio, 17
    cyclic, 17, 97
  triphosphatase, 49
  triphosphate, 16
    ATP:ADP ratio, 36
Adenyl cyclase, 97
Adipose tissue, 37, 53
Adiposity: change with aging, 23
Adrenal, 8
  androgens, 82
  cortex, 14, 81–82
Adrenergic system, 91
β-Adrenergic receptors, 50
"Adult," 7
AEP, 102–103

Age
  biologic, 115–116
    measures of, 116
  chronological, 115
  middle, 7, 115
  "spread," 22
  physiological
    battery of measurements to estimate, 115
    index of, 116
  -related changes
    in accommodation, 73
    in audible frequency, maximum, 75
    in cardiovascular system, 52
    in dorsal roots, 67
    in forced expiratory volume, 46
    in lung volume, 45
    in osmotic concentration of urine, 60
    in test meal response, 62
    in urea clearance, maximal, 60
    in ventral roots, 67
Aged, 7
  drugs and, 112–114
  pathology and, 5
Aging
  adiposity change with, 23
  body composition and, 22–27
  of body conformation, 21–22
  of brain, anatomical, 65
  cellular (see Cellular aging)
  "clock," 13
  EEG, 101–102
  free radicals and, 19–20
  genes, specific, programmed sequence in, 16
  higher functions and, 101–108

Aging (*cont.*)
  as homeostasis impairment,
    11–12
  homeostatic regulation and, 91
  as immune phenomenon, 12–13
  lipofuscin, pigment, 48
  man as special case of, 7–8
  models of, immunologic, 12
  nutrition in, 109–112
  of organ systems, 29–98
  pallor of, 37
  physical activity in, 52–54
  "pigment," 19
  population, 3
  premature, syndromes of, 16
  process, 11–20
    brain in, 5
  programmed, 17
  rate of, 5
  of reflexes, 70
  of regulatory mechanisms,
    90–98
  respiratory system in, 42–47
  of senses, 71–76
  study of (*see* Study of aging)
  theories of (*see* Theories of
    aging)
  of tissues, 29–98
Aglomerular tubular systems, 56
Air
  -alveolar interface, 44
  conduction, 74
Airway, 44
  resistance, 44
Albumin/globulin ratio, 32
Alcohol, 94
Aldosterone, 81, 96
Alimentary
  mucosa, epithelial cells of, 14
  tract, 60–63
    absorption, 63
    motility of, 61–62
    secretion and, 62–63
Alloxan, 114
Alpha rhythm, 101
Altitudes: high, acclimatization to,
    11–12

Alveolar
  air-alveolar interface, 44
  -arterial oxygen difference, 46
  bone, 39
  ducts, 42, 44
  exchange surface, 42
  $P_{o_2}$, 46
  surface area, 42
  ventilation coefficient, 53
Alveoli, 42, 44
Amino acid(s), 7
  absorption, 63
Ammonia, 59
Ammonium ion, 95
Amphetamine, 114
Amplitude, 102
Amylase: pancreatic, 63
Amyloid, 12, 67
Amylopectin, 67
Anal sphincters: internal and
    external, 62
Androgens, 86
  adrenal, 82
  excretion changes with age, 87
Anemia, 31
Angiotensin-renin system, 81, 96
Anterior chamber, 72
Antibodies: autoantibodies, 12
Antidepressants: tricyclic, 94
Antidiuretic hormone, 81
Antioxidants
  artificial, 19
  natural, 19
    vitamin E and vitamin C as,
      19
  vitamin E, 15, 19
Aorta, 114
  capacity of, 48
  size of, 48
  volume, 51
Appetite, 20, 97
Aqueous humor, 72, 74
Arcuate arteries, 56–57
Area striata, 65
Arginine
  injection of, 80
  -vasopressin, 107

Arm span, 21
Arousal, 104
Arrhythmia: atrial, 94
Arterial-alveolar oxygen difference, 46
Arteries, 48
    arcuate, 56–57
    compliance of, 48
    interlobar, 56–57
    pressure, 51, 91
    stiffness of, 48
    vertebral, 68
Arterioles
    glomerular, 59
    Isaacs-Ludwig, 56
Articular cartilage, 34
Astrocytes: fibrillary, 67
Atrial arrhythmia, 94
Atrophic gastritis, 61, 62
Atrophy: cerebral, 101
Atropine, 114
Auditory acuity: loss of, 76
Autoantibodies, 12
Autofluorescent pigment
    lipofuscin, 14
Autoimmune diseases, 12
Autonomic
    ganglia, 90
    nervous system, 6, 90–91
Averaged evoked potentials, 102–103

B

Balance, 77
Barbiturates, 114
Baroreceptor, 51
    reflex, 91
Basal
    body temperature, 93
    metabolic rate, 83, 109
Basement membrane, 33, 48–49, 57
Basilar membrane, 74
B-cells, 12
Bed: fractions of time in, for young and old persons, 103

Beta-adrenergic receptors, 50
Beta-cell, 82
    sensitivity, 82
Bicarbonate, 95
    plasma, 32
Bile, 113
Biochemical error, 18
Biofeedback, 51
Biologic age, 115–116
    measures of, 116
Biotransformation: of drugs, 112, 113
Blockade
    cholinergic, 51
    sympathetic, 51
Blood, 31–32
    cells
        red (see Red blood cell)
        white, 31–32, 60
    flow, cerebral, 51, 68
    pressure
        institutional environment and, protected, 51
        primitive societies and, 51
    volume, 31
        pulmonary capillary, 46
Body
    cell mass, 22, 25
    composition, and aging, 22–27
    conformation, aging changes in, 21–22
    fluids, volume and tonicity of, 96–97
    lean, mass, 22
    surface area, 26
    temperature, basal, 93
    water (see Water, body)
    weight, 7, 22
Bone, 33, 35
    alveolar, 39
    buffering power of, 95
    conduction, 74
    loss, 35
    marrow (see Marrow)
    mass, 35
    remodeling of, 35
Bradycardia, 50

Brain
  aging of, anatomical, 65
  in aging process, 5
  metabolic activity of, 104
  size, 5
  syndromes, chronic, 102
  weight, 7, 65
Breathing capacity: maximal, 45,
    53
Bronchial drainage, 46
Buffer
  base, 95
  capacity, total, 95
Buffering, 95
  power of bone, 95
Butylated hydroxy toluene: toluene
    derivative, 19

C

Calcification, 34
Calcitonin, 35
Calcium, 111
  ionized, 32
Caloric test, 76
Calories
  "activity," 110
  expended in physical activity,
    110
  requirement for, decreased, 110
  restriction of, 13
cAMP, 17, 97
Cancer, 12
Capillaries, 48
Cardiac (see Heart)
Cardiovascular system, 18, 48–52
  age-related changes in, 52
Caries, 38
Carotid pulse, 49
Cartilage, 33
  articular, 34
  costal, 34
  fibrocartilage, 34
  hyaline, 34
Cartilaginous articulation, 44
Cataract, 7
Catecholamines, 88
  synthesis of, 69

Cell(s)
  B-cells, 12
  beta-cell, 82
    sensitivity, 82
  blood
    red (see Red blood cell)
    white, 31–32, 60
  body, mass, 22, 25
  changes in nervous system,
    65–68
  chromophobe, 80
  cycle, prereplicative phases of,
    16
  diameter, mean, 31
  diploid, 15
  eosinophil, 80
  epithelial (see Epithelial, cells)
  fusion experiments, 16
  germ, 17
  germinal, 86
  Golgi type II, 65
  hair, 74
  intermitotic, 14
  interstitial, 57
    of Leydig, 86
  mobility, 33
  myocardial, 48
    fixed in postmitotic state, 14
  neoplastic, line of, 16
  postmitotic, 14
  pyramidal, 65
  reverting, 14
  Sertoli's, 86
  supporting, of nervous system,
    65
  T-cells, 12
    function of, 12
  transformation of, 16
  transformed, 17
Cellular aging 13–17
  "clinker" theory of, 15
  as programmed phenomenon,
    17
  study of, 15–17
  in vivo, 17
Cement substance: of root of
    tooth, 39
Centenarians, 4

Central
control sensitivity, 93
processing, 71
Cerebellum, 65, 77
Cerebral
atrophy, 101
blood flow, 51, 68
"Change of life," 88
Chest
cage, 43
circumference, 22
muscles of, 43
volume, 44
wall, compliance of, changing, 43
Chlorpromazine, 114
Cholelithiasis, 63
Choline, 107
acetyltransferase, 70
Cholinergic
blockade, 51
neurotransmitter, 106
parts, 91
receptors, 114
synapses, facilitation at, 106
Chondroitin sulfate, 33
Chorea: Huntington's, 70
Choroid plexus, 67
Chromatin, 14
Chromophobe cells, 80
Chromosomal abnormality, 84
Chronotropic response, 50
Cilia, 47
Ciliary muscle, 72
Circadian rhythm, 81
Circulation
cutaneous, 51
microcirculation, 53
splanchnic, 51
Circumvalate papillae, 40
Climacteric, 88
(See also Menopause)
female, 84
"Clinker" theory: of cellular aging, 15
Clitoris, 85
"Clock:" aging, 13
Clonus, 78

"Closing volume," 45, 46
Cochlea, 74
Coefficient: ventilatory, 114
Cognition: impaired, 107
"Cold diuresis," 94
Collagen, 19, 33, 44
Collagenase, 34
Colloid osmotic pressure, 32
Colonic dysfunction, 61
Compliance
of arteries, 48
changing, of lung and thoracic wall, 43
reduction of, 53
total, 44
"Concentration," 107
Conditioning
physical, 51
programs, 53
tranquilizing effect of, 54
Conduction
air, 74
bone, 74
velocity, 68
in ulnar nerve, and age, 68
Conjugation, 113
Connective tissues, 33–35
ground substance of, 33
mucopolysaccharides of, 19
Constipation, 61, 111
Contractility: of cardiovascular system, 48
Contraction: tertiary, and esophagus, 61
Control sensitivity: central, 93
"Convenience foods," 109
Core temperature, 92
Corium, 37
Corpora
amylacea, 67, 86
lutea, 84
Corpus striatum, 69
Corpuscular volume: mean, 31
Cortical inhibition, 107
Corticosterone, 13
Corticotropin, 81
Costal cartilage, 34
Coupling time, 50

Creatine phosphate, 36
Creatinine, 32, 60
Cristae, 14
  ampullaris, 76
"Critical fusion frequency," 74
Cross-linkage, 33
Cross-linking, 19
Culture: in vitro, 15
Cutaneous (*see* Skin)
Cytoplasts, 16

D

Death
  entropy, 6
  eugeric, 6
  genes, 17
  natural, 6
  premature, 5
Defense
  mechanisms of immune system,
    11
  systems, 11
Dehydration, 96
Delta
  activity, high-voltage, 104
  frequencies, 101–102
  rhythm, 104
Dementia, 101
  senile, 66, 70
Demographic data, 3
"Denervation hypersensitivity," 90
Dental
  hygiene, 38
  pulp, 39
Dentin, 38
Dexamethasone test, 81
Diabetes mellitus: adult-onset, 82
Diaphragm, 43
Diarrhea, 96
Diastolic pressure, 51
Diet: secular changes in, 10
Differentiating intermitotic cells,
    14
Diffusing capacity, 46, 95
Diffusion impairment, 46
Diodrast, 58
2:3 Diphosphoglycerate, 47

Diploid cells, 15
Discharge: synchrony of, 103
Disease processes: overwhelming
    defense or repair systems, 5
Disks: intervertebral, 34
Distensibility: of cardiovascular
    system, 48
Diuresis: "cold," 94
Diuretics, 97
Diurnal variation, 81
Diverticulosis, 61
DNA, 17
  errors and, 17
  repair and life span, 18
L-Dopa, 69
Dopamine, 69
Dorsal roots
  aging change in, 67
  lumbosacral, 67
Down's syndrome, 17
DPG, 47
2:3 DPG, 53
Dreaming, 105
  "sleep," 105
Dromotropy, 50
Drugs
  absorption of, 112
  adverse reactions to, 112
  aged and, 112–114
  biotransformation, 112, 113
  clearance of, 113–114
  distribution of, volume, 112, 113
  dynamics of, changes in, 114
  elimination of, 112, 113
  interaction with target tissues,
    114
  kinetics of, 112
    changes in, 114
  pharmacodynamics, 112
  transport of, 112–113
  volatile, 114
D-xyloase, 63
Dysmetria, 77

E

Eccrine sweat glands, 37
ECG, 49

EEG: aging, 101–102
"Elastic recoil," 43
Elasticity, 43
  of cardiovascular system, 48
Elastin, 19, 33, 34, 44
Elderly (see Aged)
Electrocardiography, 49
Electroencephalography: aging,
    101–102
Electromyography, 36, 68, 71
EMG, 102
EMS, 49
Enamel, 38
End-diastolic volume, 49
Endocrine system, 80–84, 90
Endoplasmic reticulum: rough, 14
Energy cost, 53
Engram, 105
Entropy, 6
  death, 6
Environment: internal, and
    homeostasis, 11
Enzyme(s), 17
  systems, 53
    microsomal, 113
    thiol-dependent, 19
Eosinophil cells, 80
Epithelial
  cells, 60
    of alimentary mucosa, 14
    turnover rate of, 61
  layer of skin, 37
Epithelium of gum: stratified, 39
Erections, 105
Error theory of aging, 17–18
Erythroblast, 14
Erythrocyte
  (See also Red blood cell)
  sedimentation rate, 31
Escalator: "mucus," 47
Esophagus, 61
  motility, 109
  sphincter
    lower, 61, 109
    upper, 61
  tertiary contractions and, 61
Estrogen, 35, 85, 86
  deficiency, 88

excretion, 87
  changes with age, 87
Eugeric death, 6
Excitation: of myocardium, 50
Expiratory volume
  reserve, 43, 44
  timed force, 116
Eye: lens of, protein of, 7

F

Failure
  redundancy, 18
  repair, 18
Fallopian tubes, 85
Fast activity, 101
Fat
  -free mass, 22
  -soluble vitamins, 111
Fatty acids: essential, 111
Feedback
  negative, 11
  systems, 11
    of hypothalamus and pituitary,
      80
Fenestrations: of endothelium, 49
Fiber, 111
Fibrillation: ventricular, 94
Fibrinogen, 32
Fibroblasts, 15, 33
Fibrocartilage, 34
Filiform papillae, 40
Filtration fraction, 58
Flow
  rate, mid-expiratory, 45
  shunt, 46
Fluid(s)
  body, volume and tonicity of,
    96–97
  extracellular, 24
  intracellular, 24
Food
  additive, 19
  "convenience," 109
  intake, reduction of, 20
Forced expiratory volume, 44–45
  age-related change in, 46
Fovea, 74

Fragility, 31
Free radicals (*see* Radicals, free)
Frequencies
    audible, maximum, age-related
        change in, 75
    perceivable, 74
Functional residual capacity, 43,
    44, 46, 114

G

GABA 70
Gait, 77
Gamma-aminobutyric acid, 70
Ganglia, 91
    autonomic, 90
    basal, 67
        dopamine in, 69
Ganglionic synapses, 90
Gastric
    emptying time, 61
    glands, 63
    secretion, 62
Gastritis: atrophic, 61, 62
Genes
    aging, specific, programmed
        sequence in, 16
    death, 17
Germ cells, 17
Germinal cells, 86
Gingiva, 39
Globulin, 32
    /albumin ratio, 32
Glomerular
    arterioles, 59
    capillary loops, 56
    filtration rate, 58, 95, 97, 113
        decline in, 58
Glomeruli, 56
    juxtamedullary, 56
Glucagon, 82
Glucocorticoid(s)
    as immunosuppressive, 13
    levels, plasma, 81
Glucose, 59
    clamp technique, 82
    level, blood, 11
    reabsorption and kidney tubules,
        57

tolerance, 82
    curve, 82
Glutamic acid, 70
    decarboxylase, 70
Glutamine, 96
Glycogen, 16, 36
Glycoprotein, 33
Golgi type II cells, 65
Gonadotropins, 84
    excretion changes with age, 87
    pituitary, 86
    releasing factors, 69
Graft vs. host reaction, 12
Granulocytes, 32
Granulovacuolar degeneration, 66
Gravity: specific, 22, 24
Gray matter
    changes, 65
    loss, differing rates of, 66
Graying of hair, 116
    axillary, 38
Growth, 20
    hormone, 13, 80, 88
    "late," 21
    of nails, 38
    period, 7
Guanine monophosphate, 16
    cAMP:cGMP ratio, 17
    rise in, 17
Gum, 39
Gustatory sensation, 40
Gut motility, 111
Gyrus, 65
    postcentral, 65, 76
    precentral, 65
    temporal, superior, 65

H

$H^+$ ion, 96
Hair
    axillary, 38
    cells, 74
    graying of, 116
        axillary, 38
    loss, 38
    pubic, 38, 85
Half-life, 113
Haversian canals, 35

Hearing, 74–75
Heart, 48–52
  aged, and tilting, 51
  cycle, 49
  output, 50, 53
    propranolol reducing, 114
    resting, changing in, 50
  rate, 11, 49, 50, 91
    maximum, 50
    maximum, decrease with
      aging, 47
  sounds, 49
  weight, 48
  work, 51
    peripheral resistance and, 51
Heat
  loss, evaporative, 92
  production, basal, 92
Height
  loss of, 21
  age of onset, 21
  sitting, 21
Hematocrit value, 31
Hemispheric volume, 65
Hemocytoblasts, 14
Hemoglobin concentration, 31, 47
Hemopoiesis, 32
Hepatocyte, 14
Hexamethonium, 91
Higher functions: and aging,
  101–108
Hindbrain: norepinephrine in, 69
Hippocampus, 66
Hiroshima, 116
Homeostasis, 6
  acid-base, 60
  aging as impairment of, 11–12
  competence, 6, 80
  control, 8
  internal environment and, 11
  mechanisms of, aging of, 91–97
  regulation of, and aging, 91
Homeothermy, 92
Hormone(s)
  antidiuretic, 81
  growth, 13, 80, 88
  "killer," 18
  parathormone, 35, 59, 83
  reproductive, 86–88

sex, 13, 86
thymic, fractions of, 13
thymosin, 13
thyroid, 18
Host: graft vs. host reaction, 12
"Hot flushes," 88
Humoral factor, 17
Huntington's chorea, 70
Hyaline cartilage, 34
Hyaluronic acid, 33
Hydrolysis, 113
Hydroxylated vitamin $D_3$, 35
Hydroxyproline, 34
Hygiene: dental, 38
Hyperemia, 51
Hyperplasia, 56
Hypersensitivity
  delayed, 13
  "denervation," 90
  in T-cell function tests, 12
Hyperthermia, 93–94
Hypertrophy, 48, 56
  compensatory, 56
  prostatic, 86
Hypoglycemia: insulin, 80
"Hypokinetic disease," 53
Hypophyseal-hypothalamo axis: for
  vasopressin, 96
Hypotension: orthostatic, 91
Hypothalamus, 13, 67
  feedback systems of, 80
  -hypophyseal axis for
    vasopressin, 96
  neurosecretion, 69
  -pituitary axis, 13
  releasing factor, 83
Hypothermia, 93–94
  "accidental," 94
Hypoxia, 51

I

Immune
  phenomenon, aging as, 12–13
  system, 12, 13, 18
    defense mechanisms of, 11
Immunodeficiency, 13
Immunologic
  efficiency, 12

Immunologic (*cont.*)
  models of aging, 12
Immunosuppressive:
  glucocorticoids as, 13
Inclusions: neurofibrillary, 101
Index: of physiologic age, 116
Infections, 12
Information
  processing of, 102
    into memory, model for, 106
  sensory, 105
  storage of, 102
  transmission of, 102
Inhibitory input, 103
Inotropic state: of myocardium, 49
Institutional environment:
  protected, and blood
    pressure, 51
Insulin, 13, 82
  hypoglycemia, 80
Intelligence quotient, 102
Interlobar arteries, 56–57
Intermitotic cells, 14
Interpleural space: potential, 42
Interstitial
  cells, 57
    of Leydig, 86
  degeneration, 67
Intervertebral disks, 34
Intima, 48
Intra-abdominal pressure, 44
Intraocular pressure, 72
IQ, 102
Iron, 63, 111
  absorption impairment, 111
Isaacs-Ludwig arteriole, 56
Ischemic attack: transient, 68
Isoproterenol, 91, 114
Isothenuria, 59

K

K⁺, exchangeable
  changing ratio and, 25
  course of, 26
Kidney, 56–60, 113
  collecting ducts, 97
  concentrating ability, 57, 59

juxtamedullary units, 56
mass, 57–58
  decline in, 57
  medulla, 56, 97
  osmotic stratification process,
    57
  perfusion, 58, 113
    rate, decline in, 58
  proximal convoluted segment,
    56
  tubules, 56
    glucose reabsorption and, 57
  systems, aglomerular, 56
  veins, 57
  weight, 57
Kinetics of drugs: changes in, 114
Kraus end organs, 72

L

Labia, 85
"Late growth," 21
Latency, 102
  fibroblast culture and, 16
L-dopa, 69
Lean mass
  body, 22
  muscle, 53
Learning, 102, 105–107
  peripheral, 107
Lecithin, 107
Leg length, 21
Lens, 72
  protein of, 7
Leukocytes, 31–32, 60
Lewy bodies, 66
Leydig: interstitial cells of, 86
Life
  expectancy, 3, 4
  postreproductive, 8
  span, 4, 7, 17, 31, 109
    DNA repair and, 18
  potential, 4, 5–7
  potential, maximal, 5
  -style, 7
    secular changes in, 10
Ligament: periodontal, 39
Limbic system, 67

Lipase: pancreatic, 63
Lipids, 16
  absorption, 63
  peroxidation, 19
Lipofuscin, 66
  pigment
    aging, 48
    autofluorescent, 14
    varieties of, 15
Lipoprotein
  high density, 32
  low density, 32
Liver: biotransformation in, 113
Locus ceruleus, 65
Long-lived special groups: in
    Ecuador and Georgian
    Russia, 7
Lumbosacral dorsal roots, 67
Lung, 34, 113
  blood volume, capillary, 46
  compliance of, changing, 43
  as compliant, 43
  volume
    age-related changes in, 45
    total, 42
Lunula, 38
LVET, 49
Lymph nodes, 12
Lymphocyte production, 32
T-Lymphocytes, 17
Lymphoid tissue, 12
Lysosomes, 15, 16, 19

M

Macrophages, 47
Macula, 76
Malnutrition, 109
Malonaldehyde, 19
Mammary glands, 85
MAO, 69
  inhibitors, 69
Marrow, 12
  red, 32
  yellow, 32
Maturation, 20
  period, 109
Maximal breathing capacity, 45, 53

Maximum
  heart rate, 50
  isometric tension, 49
Meal, test, 62
  response to, age-related changes
    in, 62
Mean
  cell diameter, 31
  corpuscular volume, 31
Measurements: battery of, to
    estimate physiological age,
    115
Meissner's corpuscles, 71
Melanophore activity, 37
Membrane potential: resting, 36
Memory, 102, 105-107
  consolidation of, 105
  formation, 105
  function, 107
  long-term, 105, 106
  processing of information into,
    model for, 106
  recognition, 106
  short-term, 105, 106
  -specific peptides, 106
Menarche, 84
Menopause, 35, 80, 84, 88
  (See also Climacteric)
Menstrual cycle, 84
Mental impairment, 102
"Metabolic repair," 104
Metabolism, 109
  rate of, 7, 18
Metacarpals: radiographic density
    of, 116
Microcirculation, 53
Microopacities, 72
Microsomal enzyme systems, 113
Microtubules, 66
Middle-age, 7, 115
  "spread," 22
Mid-expiratory flow rate, 45
Minerals, 111
Miniature end plate potentials, 36
Mitochondria, 14, 19, 48
Mitosis, 14
Model(s)
  immunologic, of aging, 12

Model(s) *(cont.)*
  for processing of information
    into memory, 106
Monoamine oxidase, 69
  inhibitors, 69
Monosynaptic reflexes, 70
Morbidity: compression of, 6
Mortality *(see* Death)
Motility: of alimentary tract,
    61–62
Motion sickness, 77
Motoneurons, 36
Motor
  end plate, 36
  function, 61
  "time," 71
  units, 36
Mouth, 38–40
Mucin secretion, 40
Mucopolysaccharides, 33
  of connective tissue, 19
"Mucus escalator," 47
Multisynaptic pathways, 69
Muscarinic terminations, 91
Muscle(s), 36–37
  ciliary, 72
  contraction period, 37
  fibers, 36
  force of myocardium, 49
  latent period, 37
  mass, 36
    lean, 53
  peak tension, 37
  power, 3
  red, 36
  relaxation period, 37
  respiratory, 44
  skeletal, 14
  strength, 37
  of thorax, 43
Myelin, 65
Myocardium, 48, 49
  cells of, 48
    fixed in postmitotic state, 14
  excitation of, 50
  inotropic state of, 49
  muscle force of, 49

relaxation time, 49
  velocity of shortening in aging,
    49
Myofibrils, 36, 49
Myxedema, 38

N

Nail
  growth, 38
  longitudinal ridges in, 38
Natural death, 6
"Nearpoint," 72
Negative feedback, 11
Neoplastic cell line, 16
Nephron
  distal, 95
  units, 56
Nerves
  parasympathetic, 90
  sympathetic, 90
  ulnar, conduction velocity and
    age, 68
Nervous system, 65–79
  autonomic, 6, 90–91
  cellular changes in, 65–68
  posterior column system, 66
  supporting cells, 65
Neuritic plaques, 67
Neuroaxonal degeneration, 65
Neurofibrillary
  inclusions, 101
  tangles, 66
Neurons, 65
  fixed in postmitotic state, 14
  loss of, 101
Neurosecretion: hypothalamic, 69
Neurotransmitter, 36, 68–70, 101
  cholinergic, 106
Nipples, 85
Noncarbonic acid: buffering of,
    95
Norepinephrine, 69, 91, 114
  in hindbrain, 69
Nuclear membrane, 14
Nucleoli, 14
5'-Nucleotidase, 16

Nucleus, 14, 16
pulposus, 34
Nutrition: in aging, 109–112
Nystagmus, 76

O

Obesity, 109
Odontoblast, 39
Odontoblastic activity, 39
"Old," 7
"very," 7
Olfactory
bulb, 75
sensitivity, 75
Olivodentate system, 78
Oral structures, 38–40
Organ
of Corti, supporting cell loss, 74
systems, aging of, 29–98
Orthostatic hypotension, 91
Osmotic
concentration of urine, aging
changes in, 60
pressure
colloid, 32
plasma, 32
stratification, 97
process, medullary, 57
Ossicles, 74
Osteoblastic activity, 35
Osteoclastic activity, 35
Osteoporosis, 35
postmenopausal, 83, 88
Ovary, 84
primordial follicles, 84
loss of, 85
steroids of, 88
Overnutrition, 109
Oxidation, 113
Oxidative damage: due to free
radicals, 15
Oxygen
consumption
basal, 26
maximum, decrease with
aging, 47

difference, alveolar-arterial, 46
dissociation curve, 47

P

Pacinian organs, 72
PAH, 58
Tm for, 59
Pain threshold, 72
Pallor: of aging, 37
Pancreas, 82
amylase, 63
juice, 63
lipase, 63
Papillae
circumvalate, 40
filiform, 40
Para-aminohippuric acid, 58
Parasympathetic nerves, 90
Parathormone, 35, 59, 83
Parathyroid, 83–84
Parkinsonism, 69
"Pathogeric"
causes, 5
processes, 5
Pathology: and aged, 5
Pelvic diameter, 22
PEP, 49
Pepsin secretion, 62
Perfusion, 51, 53
renal, 58
ventilation and, 114
-ventilation
imbalance, 53
relationship, 46
Periodontal
disease, 38
ligament, 39
tissues, 39
Peripheral resistance, 53, 91
Peristalsis, 61
primary, 61
Peristaltic elements: and
"presbyesophagus," 61
Peritubular plexus, 56
pH, 32, 94
Pharmacodynamics, 112

Physical
  activity
    in aging, 52–54
    calories expended in, 110
  capacity, 53
  conditioning, 51
  work capacity, 53
Physiological (*see* Age,
    physiological)
Pigment
  "aging," 19
  granules, 14
  lipofuscin (*see* Lipofuscin,
    pigment)
Pituitary, 18, 80–81
  anterior, 80
  feedback systems of, 80
  gonadotropins, 86
  -hypothalamo axis, 13
  trophic factor, 83
Plantar flexion reflexes, 70
Plaques, 101
  neuritic, 67
Plasma
  bicarbonate, 32
  membrane, 19
  osmotic pressure, 32
  protein, 112
    concentrations, 32
Platelet count, 32
Po$_2$: alveolar, 46
Polyphasic potentials, 37
  action, 68
Postmenopausal syndrome, 88
Postmitotic cell, 14
Postreproductive life, 8
Posture, 77
Potassium: exchangable, 23
Potential(s)
  action, polyphasic, 68
  averaged evoked, 102–103
  interpleural space, 42
  miniature end plate, 36
  polyphasic, 37
  resting membrane, 36
Preganglionic stimulation, 90
Premature
  aging, syndromes of, 16

death, 5
"Presbyesophagus," 61
Presbyopia, 72
Pressure
  arterial, 51
  blood (*see* Blood, pressure)
  diastolic, 51
  systolic, 51
Pre-T-cells, 12
Primitive societies: and blood
    pressure, 51
Primordial follicles of ovary,
    84
  loss of, 85
Progeria, 16
Programmed
  aging, 17
  phenomenon, cellular aging as,
    17
  sequence and specific aging
    genes, 16
Proinsulin, 82
Prolactin, 80
Propranolol: reducing heart
    output, 114
Proprioceptive
  input, 77
  sense, 72
Prostaglandins, 88
Prostate, 86
  hypertrophy, 86
Protein
  concentrations, plasma, 32
  -dating, 7
  fibrils, 66
  intracellular, 95
  of lens of eye, 7
  plasma, 112
  requirement, 110
  synthesis, 17
  tooth, 7
Pseudo-elastin, 34
Psychomotor speed, 107
Ptosis, 74
Ptyalin, 62
Puberty, 18
Pubic hair, 38, 85
Pulmonary (*see* Lung)

Pulp
cavity, 39
dental, 39
Pulse
carotid, 49
wave, velocity of, 48
Pupil, 73
Pyramidal cells, 65

R

Racemization, 7
Radicals, free
aging and, 19–20
diffusible, 19
oxidative damage to, 15
Radiographic density: of
metacarpals, 116
Rate: of aging, 5
Reaction time, 71
components of, 71
Receptor, 69
cholinergic, 114
sites, 114
Red blood cell, 31, 112
(See also Erythrocyte)
count, 31
metabolism, 47
Red marrow, 32
Red muscle, 36
Redundancy failure, 18
Reflexes
abdominal, superficial, 70
aging of, 70
baroreceptor, 91
monosynaptic, 70
plantar flexion, 70
stretch, 70
Refractory period
absolute, 37
relative, 37
Regulatory
mechanisms, aging of, 90–98
processes, 11
Reisner's membrane, 74
Relaxation techniques, 51
Remodeling: of bone, 35
Renal (see Kidney)

Renin-angiotensin system, 81, 96
Repair failure: in theories of aging,
18
"Replacement therapy," 13
Reproductive
hormones, 86–88
period, 8
system, 84–88
Residual volume, 43, 44, 46, 53
Respiratory
muscles, 44
reserve, 95
system in aging, 42–47
Resting
membrane potential, 36
tension, 49
Reticulum
endoplasmic, rough, 14
fibers of, 33, 34
Retina: peripheral, rods of, 74
Reverting cell, 14
Rhythm
alpha, 101
delta, 104
Rib cage, 43
RNA, 17, 106
errors and, 17
Rods: of peripheral retina, 74

S

Saccule, 76, 77
Salivary
glands, 40
secretion, 62
Sarcolemma, 36
Sarcomeres, 36
Sebaceous glands, 37
Secretin, 63
Secretion
acid, resting, 62
alimentary tract and, 62–63
pepsin, 62
salivary, 62
Secular changes, 8
in life-style, diet and smoking,
10
Seminal vesicles, 86

Seminiferous tubules, 86
Senility, 3
Senses
    aging of, 71–76
    cutaneous, 71–72
    proprioceptive, 72
    special, 72–76
Sensitivity
    control, central, 93
    to temperature, 72, 93
Sensory information, 105
Serotonin, 78
Sertoli's cells, 86
Sex
    hormones, 13, 86
    organs, secondary
        female, 84–85
        male, 86
    ratio in older population, 3
Shiver, 93
Shoulder width, 22
Shunt flow, 46
Sinoatrial node, 51
Sinus rhythm, 51
Sitting height, 21
Skeletal muscle, 14
Skin, 34, 37–38
    as barrier, 37
    circulation, 51
    cutaneous sense, 71–72
    -fold thickness, 22, 24
    temperature, 92, 93
    as thermal insulator, 37
Sleep, 103–104
    "dreaming," 105
    pattern, 104
    slow-wave, 80, 103
    "spindles," 104
    rapid eye movement during,
        103–104, 105
Smell, 75–76, 109
Smoking: secular changes in, 10
Social stress, 51
Sodium, exchangable, 25
    changing ratio and, 25
Sound orientation, 74
Sounds: of heart, 49
Special senses, 72–76

Species adaptation, 8
Specific gravity, 22, 24
Sperm
    count, 86
    production, 86
Spermatocyte, 14
Sphincter
    anal, internal and external, 62
    esophagus (see Esophagus,
        sphincter)
Sphincteric elements: and
        "presbyesophagus," 61
Spine: curvature of, 21
Splanchnic circulation, 51
"Splay," 59
Spleen, 12
SREM, 104, 105
SSW, 103
Starvation, 18
Stature, 8, 9
Steroids: ovarian, 88
Stomach (see Gastric)
Stratum germinativum, 37
Stress, 11
    social, 51
Stretch reflexes, 70
Stria vascularis, 74
Stroke volume, 48, 50, 51
Study of aging, 8–10
    cross-sectional study, 8
    longitudinal study, 8
    semi-longitudinal approach, 9
Substantia nigra, 69
Sulci, 65
Supporting tissues, 32–35
Surfactant, 44
Survivorship
    curve
        ideal, 6
        from 1900 to 1980
    differential, 9
Swallowing, 61
"Sway:" of body, 77
Sweat, 113
    glands, eccrine, 37
Sweating, 93, 96
Sympathetic
    blockade, 51

nerves, 90
tonus, 49
Synapses
cholinergic, facilitation at, 106
delay time, 71
ganglionic, 90
Synchrony: of discharge, 103
Systolic
pressure, 51
time intervals, 49

T

$T_3$, 83
$T_4$, 83
Tachycardia, 51
Target
temperature, 93
tissues
drug interaction with, 114
responsiveness of, 114
Taste, 75, 109
buds, 40, 75
papillae, 75
TBG, 83
T-cells, 12
function of, 12
Teeth, 38–40, 60
protein of, 7
roots of, cement substance of, 39
Temperature
"ambient," 93
basal body, 93
core, 92
high, acclimatization to, 11–12
sensitivity, 72
skin, 92, 93
target, 93
Temporal cortex, 74
Teniae coli, 61
Tension
isometric
maximum, 49
peak, 49
resting, 49
Test
caloric, 76
meal, 62

response, age-related changes
in, 62
Testis, 86
Testosterone, 86
Thebesian veins, 46
Theories of aging, 17–18
cellular aging as programmed
phenomenon, 17
error, 17–18
"killer hormone," 18
redundancy failure, 18
repair failure, 18
Thermal
comfort, 93
sensitivity, 93
Thermoregulation, 12, 37, 91–92
Theta frequencies, 101–102
Thiamine, 111
Thiol-dependent enzymes, 19
Thirst, 97
Thorax (see Chest)
Thymectomized animal, 13
Thymosin, 13
Thymus, 12, 13
hormones, fractions of, 13
involution, 12
Thyroid, 83
activity, 18
hormone, 18
Thyrotropin, 81
Thyroxin binding globulin, 83
Thyroxine, 13, 83
Tilting: and aged heart, 51
Timed
force expiratory volume, 116
ventilatory functions, 44
Tinnitus, 74
Tissues
adipose, 37
aging of, 29–98
connective (see Connective
tissues)
periodontal, 39
target (see Target, tissues)
"Titratable acidity," 59, 95
Tm: for PAH, 59
Toluene derivative butylated
hydroxy toluene, 19

Trace elements, 111
Tranquilizing effect: of
    conditioning, 54
Transformation: of cells, 16
Transformed cells, 17
Transplantation, 15
Tremor, 77–78
    "intention," 77
    "physiologic," 78
    resting, 77
TRH, 83
Tricyclic antidepressants, 94
Triiodothyronine, 83
Tropocollagen, 33
Trunk length, 21
Trypsin, 63
TSH, 83
T-tubule system, 36
Tubules
    distal, 97
    of kidney (see Kidney, tubules)
    seminiferous, 86
Tunica media, 48
Tympanic membrane, 74


U

Ulnar nerve: conduction velocity,
        and age, 68
Urea, 32
    clearance, 59
        maximal, aging changes in, 60
Uric acid, 32
Urinary cation, 95
Urine: osmotic concentration of,
        age changes in, 60
Uterus, 84
Utricle, 76, 77


V

Vagal recruitment, 51
Vagina, 85
    lining of, 85
Valsalva maneuver, 91
Vasa recta, 56
Vascular (see Vessels)

Vasopressin, 59, 81, 96, 97
    arginine-, 107
    hypothalamo-hypophyseal axis
        for, 96
Vegetative intermitotic cells, 14
Veins, 48
    renal, 57
    thebesian, 46
Ventilation
    coefficient, 114
        alveolar, 53
    perfusion and, 114
    -perfusion
        imbalance, 53
        relationship, 46
Ventilatory capacity, 53
Ventral roots: aging change in, 67
Ventricle, 65
    fibrillation, 94
Verbal function, 102
Vertebral arteries, 68
Vessels, 48–52
    disease, 101
Vestibular
    apparatus, 76
    function, 76–77
    input, 77
Vibratory threshold, 72
Viscosity, 31
Vision, 72–74
Visual
    acuity, 3, 74
    field, 74
    threshold, 73
Vital capacity, 42, 53
Vitamins
    A, 111
    $B_1$, 63
    $B_{12}$, 63, 111
    B-group, 111
    C, 111
        as natural antioxidant, 19
    D, 111
    $D_3$, hydroxylated, 35
    E, as antioxidant, 15
        natural, 19
    fat-soluble, 111
    supplementation of, 111

Vitreous body, 73
Volume
    aortic, 51
    blood, 31
        pulmonary capillary, 46
    "closing," 45, 46
    end-diastolic, 49
    expiratory
        forced, 44–45
        forced, age-related change in, 46
        reserve, 43, 44
        timed force, 116
    hemispheric, 65
    lung (*see* Lung, volume)
    residual, 43, 44, 46, 53
    stroke, 48, 50, 51
    thoracic, 44

## W

Water, body
    extracellular component of, 32
    total, 22, 23
Wave: pulse, velocity of, 48

Weight
    body, 7, 22
    brain, 7
White blood cells, 31–32, 60
White matter
    changes, 65
    loss, differing rates of, 66
"Windkessel," 35
Work
    of heart, 51
        peripheral resistance and, 51
    physical, capacity for, 53
Wrinkling, 37

## Y

Yellow marrow, 32
"Young," 7

## Z

Zona
    fasciculata, 81
    glomerulosa, 96
    reticularis, 14